Practitioner Soci

Practitioner Social Work Research in Action

edited by

Bob Broad & Colin Fletcher

Whiting and Birch Ltd

MCMXCIII

Published by Whiting & Birch Ltd, PO Box 872, Forest Hill, London
SE23 3HL, England.
USA: Paul & Co, Publishers' Consortium Inc, PO Box 442, Concord, MA 01742.

British Library Cataloguing in Publication Data.
A CIP catalogue record is available from the British Library

ISBN 1 871177 62 6 (cased)
ISBN 1 871177 63 4 (limp)

Printed in England by Bourne Press Limited, Bournemouth

CONTENTS

Editors' Acknowledgements

This book owes its existence to Cranfield's Department of Social Policy (1974-1992) and particularly to the work of John Brown, John Paley, Philip Topping, Jim Thomas and Graham Howes.

The contributors, themselves, have engaged in a lengthy process with good natured patience. Selina Cook prepared draft after draft and Louise Gadd polished off the final version. Our heartfelt thanks to all these good colleagues.

It is hard to improve on Victor Borge's acknowledgement at the beginning of his performances. He thanked 'my parents for making it possible and my children for making it necessary'. It also goes without saying that all the mistakes are somebody else's and all the good bits belong to the authors.

Introduction

This book sets out to highlight the research contributions which can be made by practitioners in the varied field of social work. Each piece embraces a distinct topic yet all are united by their author's desire to go beyond stated agency objectives and superficialities, get beneath the surface, and improve client delivery systems. All pieces, too, combine two elements; that relating to the subject matter in hand (for example Special Education, or Probation), and that relating to methodological issues and fieldwork.

The contributions are segments taken from the author's postgraduate thesis, based on their successful completion of a research project, and undertaken and supervised at Cranfield Institute of Technology's Social Policy Department between 1981-1991. The course's qualification was upgraded from MSc to MPhil in 1984-1985. The authors took time out, on a part or full time basis, from their social work job to undertake the research and submit it for examination. The contributions were initially submitted to us by the authors themselves and then selected within our own brief of obtaining quality material which could be readily edited into article length without that quality being compromised.

The contributors were asked to choose a favourite part of their thesis. These selections were edited first by Bob Broad then by Colin Fletcher and sent back to authors for alterations and acceptance. Bob and Colin are the practitioner/researcher and researcher/practitioner respectively, their working relationship began as student and tutor. They had been attracted by practitioner research both as an ideal and as an invitation to innovate. This book is an exploration of the issues which they and fellow partners face in doing practitioner research. The practitioner research for a higher degree, whilst built on themes and knowledge common to other sorts of research, is also distinct from them in several ways:

1. In most cases practitioners volunteer to attend the course, with their own plans about what to research or may, carry forward their employers ideas about what to research.
2. The researchers are trained social workers and have research training whilst also undertaking the research project.
3. The research is supervised by a person with considerable research skills.

4. The research is subject to strict time limits about thesis submission.
5. The research will only pass if it is up to post-graduate standard.

It is these characteristics of postgraduate practitioner research; the independence, its pressure and quality restraints, the practitioner's training status, high self motivation, and ambition that can combine to produce tensions. Nicki Cornwell's piece is an example of a practitioner discovering an important and sensitive topic to research and then having to negotiate and renegotiate, formally and informally, access to the fieldwork. Other tensions relate to the practitioner's voyage of enquiry with its seemingly intrinsic elements of doubt and uncertainty.

In relation to these elements David Bowen's application of the life history approach (for school non-attenders), Mike Carpenter's use of the panel study (for evaluating social work assessments) and Bob Broad's use of sociograms as a way of understanding about activity groups in Probation are good examples. Strong support for practitioners to experiment with a wide range of research methodologies is a key factor. Yet more 'conventional' research methods can, of course, also produce significant findings and in this respect David Bamber's writing about social work and the roles of tutors' training is revealing. Each piece illustrates that with proper guidance, a creative imagination and rigorous skills, practitioner research can and does make a significant contribution to both the knowledge and application of social work.

What of the future for the format of practitioner research described in this book? In a hostile economic climate the opportunities for specialist social work research positions are extremely limited, and in some fields, almost non-existent. There is an increasing tendency for short term project funding and not for long term research post funding.

There are strict economies and calls for partnership research between and across different organisations and interests. Despite the economic necessities and reasoning behind it, partnership in small scale research which is not directly government funded combines well with the practitioner research framework, and could emerge as a potent force in the future. Practitioner research may develop outside an academic-practice partnership and inside an organisation through research which is answerable only to employers runs the risk of being less enquiring and less open about unpopular findings. So far a sort of academic quality threshold has been developed at Cranfield and elsewhere. The university base of practitioner research is growing and includes, in Britain, the Universities of Dundee, Leicester and Stirling. Charitable trusts too, we feel, are increasingly likely to fund practitioner research.

Calls for effectiveness of service delivery, equal opportunities, and quality control in social work appear three of the key research areas for the 1990s and beyond. It is likely that future practitioner research will more clearly represent and highlight those concerns and interests.

It is well placed to do so provided that social work employers when faced with complex social work issues do not expect a 'quick fix' and instant answers but are prepared to fund and respond to practitioner research.

•

The book opens with an analysis of practitioner research and closes with two reflections on the collective experiences. The other parts are based upon our analysis of the articles' main emphases: surveys; investigations; appraisals and innovations, finishing with a practitioner's cautionary tale. We do not labour these sorts of study or seek to prove their individual ingenuities and importances. With hindsight, there have been these four kinds of practitioner research to date. With foresight we can imagine these particular kinds continuing and yet being merged by some and added to by others. Thus the concluding analysis *of* practitioner research is taken forward to an agenda *for* practitioner research. We can foresee practitioner research becoming firmly rooted in post-qualifying education and so gaining a growing influence upon initial training.

Bob Broad and Colin Fletcher
1993

Part One
Reflecting on an Experience

An Analysis of Practitioner Research

COLIN FLETCHER

An Origin

Practitioner research, in England, was 'invented' by John Brown in 1974. He thought there should be a partnership in higher education between experienced professionals in the public sector and experienced researchers. His ideas were to bring together the professionals' concerns and the researchers' competences: to do a distinctive kind of study and to write about it in an equally distinctive way. He took no interest in post qualifying training. That, we shall see, is a development which is only just beginning.

John Brown's early career was as a linguist, an adult educator on community health in the West Indies and as Warden of a Hall of Residence. In each sphere he thought about local culture and befriended local professionals. His conversations led him to want to encourage professionals to follow their insights and intuitions. At Cranfield Institute, he was himself busy doing community studies in the nearby and multi-racial town of Bedford. Before long he created a Masters Degree in Practitioner Research through which professionals could express their concerns and engage in a range of established research methods and so find ones which suited their needs. The course was for inter-professional, interdisciplinary and applied research.

A Question of Timing

There is a right time for practitioner research. The right time is when, after initial training and qualification and some years of experience, a professional feels ready for another substantial step. This professional can say:

- My profession is worthy and honourable.
- I am good at my job.
- I intend to stick at it.
- I have doubts and difficulties about the way things are going.

- I am ready for a fresh challenge which involves stepping back to reflect and stepping forward to find out more.
- I have courage and can write.
- I don't want to change jobs just yet.
- I could do with some variety and with career enhancement.
- In my personal life I have most, or all, of the support which I need.

The professional is ready to answer some questions and so make an initial research proposal. The questions can look like this:

- What is the subject of the research?
- What are the background problems/concerns?
- What information does the research seek?
- What is the relevance to policy/practice?

With these personal thoughts and tentative answers to these research questions the practitioner is ready to consider the possibilities.

Distinctiveness

Practitioner research parallels academic research but is steadfastly different from it when in an idealised form. The comparison is not intended to be hostile rather it shows how 'closeness to the problem' shapes the perspectives of practitioner research.

Table 1
Perspectives and Their Correspondences

Perspectives	Academic Research	Practitioner Research
1. Issues	Theoretical problem	Practical problem.
2. Question	Why is it so?	How can it change?
3. Fieldwork	Impersonal methods	Personal and professional involvements.
4. Content	Politics peripheral	Politics central.
5. Resources	Journals and texts	Handbooks, packs, stories, media.
6. Connections made with	Concepts	Social forces and legislation.
7. Purpose	Illumination and proof	Arguments and recommendations

In practice, as always, there is begging, borrowing and interchange. Most practitioners believe that they have to do academic things and this belief usually makes them have a need to 'stay cool' and a wary unease of doing the 'wrong thing'. Practitioners are encouraged by the thought of doing something relevant and useful and yet worried, quite rightly, about being sufficiently rigorous. Each makes a journey trying to hold relevance in one hand and rigour in the other. The journey begins with trying to get the 'problem' clear enough to be studied effectively in the brief time which is available.

Types of Opening Questions

Practitioners' initial problem statements usually come in one of four types, these were the basis of arranging the contributions to this book:

- *a state of the art review*
  What's going on about...? (often the impact of legislation)
- *an investigation*
  what do we know very little about...? (often clients)
- *an appraisal*
  how can the methods used be improved...?
  (often concerned with a new technique)
- *an innovation*
  how can a change be accomplished...?
  (often against professional prejudices)

Quite naturally when made aware of choices such as these practitioners may prefer to address two, three or even all four! The research skill which is then most appropriate is to see the initial problem as 'a window as well as a wall', as a way through to others as well as a 'thing' in itself. They are, in part, related anyway. The first and the last (review and innovation) are linked through a common concern with development and the structural difficulties which are likely to occur. The two in between, investigation and appraisal, have a common concern with deficit or deficiency and the attitudinal deterrents which oppose reforms.

These concerns with development or deficiency, structures or attitudes do tend to remain consistently with the practitioner. They become like a silver thread running through the research. They give an indication of both the tone and the tasks of subsequent field work. The partner-researcher (the supervisor or tutor or 'critical friend') has to acknowledge the practitioner's entitlement to their initial problem statement. The practitioner, quite properly, dominates this first step of the process.

Political Feelings

Practitioners have a 'silver thread' through their themes: they should always be able to return to their initial problem when in doubt. They also have the ball and chain of an obsessive language. Generally they believe that technical language is superior and required - even if they do not use or like it themselves.

Students usually read text books. The established practitioner though does not read much apart from technical reports and light relief. A taken-for-granted truth has settled: jargon equals job, readable materials (novels and newspapers) equal leisure. Inside the jargon are acronyms as well as neologisms all of which tend to bar the way to a clear problem statement. There is an urgent need for a forum in which plain language can be used. At this point, if not earlier, the politics of the research is felt. Politics with a capital 'P' has to do with the party political content of legislation which the practitioner researcher may hope to propose, oppose, modify or exploit at the edges of its implications. Politics with a small 'p' is a 'jostling for position': they and other professionals bear their roles as both swords and shields. There is a frustration and fascination with the politics of either kind.

Political feelings run high in practitioner research. They have to be evaluated and re-evaluated. One reason for this re-evaluation is that research creates two new statuses for the practitioner. The first is the 'outside - insider', the person who (at study or at work) is clearly reflecting beyond the immediate and formal responsibilities. The second is being a 'policymaker-in-the-making' which psychologically promotes the practitioner-researcher, - they sometimes sound as if they are taking responsibility for policy. As a rule they can have a hard time `gaining access' to professionals and an easier time researching on `clients'.

A Rationale

Practitioner research in social work probably dates to 1980 with Katherine M. Wood's (1980) article 'Experiences in Teaching the Practitioner-Researcher Model'. She writes that its rationale is accountability and `at least as important'... the need to develop the empirical base for social work practice theory'. Wood seeks a balance between 'practice wisdom' and 'empirical knowledge'.

For example:

...(an) early emphasis on the process of definition, involving skills in observation (p.18)

...the practice and research processes...(being)...theory-free (pp.18-19)

...he definition of a treatment strategy as an interventive hypothesis (p.19)

The language of these principles is 'scientific' but the actions are different from 'theory to hypothesis to test' schemes of work. The essence is to redress the balance in favour of a firm recognition of 'practice wisdom'.

Some would claim that practitioner research makes a new kind or paradigm of knowledge. I would claim that there could be a greater ethical value in trying to find out 'real' acts and actions. But practitioner research need not assemble a corpus of knowledge. Rather it makes connections between what is happening and what could happen: with how practice, by definition, can always be purged, cleansed and improved. The rationale of practitioner research is that of continuous reform by professionals who have insights and influence in a democratically accountable practice.

The Choice of Methods

If current or intended practice defines the problem then the question may, at first sight, look naive and over ambitious. Such would be the case if the attempt subsequently were to answer it all. That is where refinement comes in and so is where 'methods' really need to be searching and ingenious. Again the practitioner-researcher is asking where would I go to find out, who would I ask and most importantly what corroboration would I need?

Superficially, then, practitioner research licences imaginative methods. But this is actually where being 'theory-free' really matters most. The choice is more than between quantitative and qualitative methods: the same researcher might computer analyse a questionnaire, devise and observe a training session and tape half a dozen life-stories. Any group of students can include behaviourists, literatists and feminists. Practitioners researchers need to see that there are many, many methods, all equally at their disposal. Each method has its conditions to satisfy, its quirks and its parts to be sceptical about. Methods can be elegant and able to release a lot of energy or authoritative or exploratory. Any method has to 'feel good' to its subjects who voluntarily engage and has to be efficient because there is so little time.

No practitioner-researcher is likely to believe that there is a method without snags - if there were everyone would be using it! So what is available, what has been both strong and subtle in other fields and would it be easier to invent something which might work?

I would not claim that all practitioners are methodologically creative. Those concerned with 'state of the art reviews' are likely to be creative only in devising a framework and the choice of particular questions and in deploying responses. Even so this 'only likely' can be demanding as Bernard Webb's article shows - the practitioner-researcher often uses a combination of methods and tries to get at, what is happening from different angles. The idea of 'triangulation' in Glazer and Strausse (1967) *The Discovery of Grounded Theory* is very helpful because it encourages practitioner researchers not to put 'all their eggs in one basket'. The practitioner-researcher benefits most from 'data-rich' methods, from devising their own test or observation schedule and from seeing familiar situations through the eyes of others be the others 'specialists', 'supervisors' or 'subjects'. It is the relaxed attitude to method which lends itself to creativity in method as with Cath McGaskill's *Family Fun Sheet*. Professional researchers are likely to be much more excited about this creativity than practitioner-researchers. For them methods usually feel like specialised equipment needed when at close quarters with the woodlands (or jungle!) of where action really takes place. They are regularly and modestly surprised when methodologists get excited. They see the practical value of their eventual instruments, methodologists are more aware of the potential for adoption in further studies.

Relevant Literature

Practitioner-researchers face many problems with 'the literature'. To begin with the research question is usually 'hot' - up to the minute and what should happen next. The 1980s at Cranfield, for example, opened with training needs and anti-racism, continued with modes of assessment, moved on to care in the community particularly of the elderly and then to child and elderly abuse. Each change was prompted by a professional response to new legislation *and* by professional insights into perennial problems that could be tackled in a fresh way *and* by current `crises'.

So professional or trade literature is important, as are government publications and media coverage of critical events. If writing has not appeared in professional journals practitioner-researchers often ask 'Have I got enough references?', 'Can I use bits from this pamphlet?' and 'Where can I find anything at all?!'. Two replies are possible. First written material is data as much as it is authority, it can be used in support of your *own* argument. Secondly publications of all kinds will appear whilst the research is underway. If the problem statement has been achieved by one person there is a good probability that others have been working on it too. Practitioner research 'comes on stream'. When the initial problem is defined it may seem as if no one else knows or cares beyond saying 'that's interesting'. By the time the research has been done and is being written up it may seem as if lots of people had the same idea!

The key or common principle, it seems, is to refine the initial problem *with* rather than *from* the literature and to accept that all references quoted were truly related to the research rather than packed in to give a good impression of having been busy in the library. All the same practitioners are often surprised by how much they have read by the end and how much more they would like to read in the future. Practitioners do learn to enjoy a dialogue with the literature.

Writing Styles

Reading the literature regularly bewilders the practitioner about what are the acceptable styles of writing. There is the pull of academicism, the push of journalism and the pressure of 'officialese'. Sometimes practitioners are frightened of writing in readable prose, they fear exposure and being 'lightweight'. Their greatest difficulty is to resolve who the writing is for. They would like professional colleagues to enjoy it, they would like academics to engage in the ideas and they would like to inform politicians and policymakers on important matters.

The writing of the report, study or dissertation is therefore best done as one step is left for the next. Then it becomes apparent that there are different languages, or at least dialects being learned, and used to the best of one's ability. Practitioner-researchers rarely have a set and single style to begin with: a few are naturals but most are stilted.

What makes a natural is the feeling that their work is original and genuine, there is 'no axe to grind' and are no 'ghosts' in their mental machinery. The effort is to take time to be clear, use small (ish) sentences and reserve rather than rush to judgement. Chapters do not come easily and may resemble whole books at first. Nevertheless working within a frame is better than struggling with an interminable splurge. Very few practitioners like their style and most only come to appreciate it after editing earlier drafts and being `well on' with their writing. A style develops but almost any style will do to begin with! Regular writing episodes help to build up achievements and fit the research into a busy schedule. Invariably practitioner-researchers are also surprised with how much they have written and with the warm appreciation of their readers.

Practice Wisdom

A practitioner-researcher is a person working as a professional who relates their learning to the pressures and possibilities of the job and who gains 'practice-wisdom' from colleagues.

'Practice-wisdom' can be a good, bad or indifferent thing. It is good when insights and evaluations flow from reflection about current actions. It is bad when habits ossify to the extent that 'clients' become 'cannon-fodder'. It is indifferent when it relates to administrative and paperwork activities whose function is to 'just keep the job going'. Professional and practitioner may be said, at times, to be greater or less than each other. Professional is greater when referring to ethics or values that are higher than commercial or personal gain. Practitioner is greater when good 'practice-wisdom' grants sufficient autonomy to be able to act upon and alter the profession. All the same practitioner research is not in an antagonistic relationship with being a professional. It is an additional and active expression which helps to avoid, as Wood says, the professional tumbling into a technician role. Practitioner research is in both a defensive and developmental relationship with professionalism. Practitioner-researchers want to make the most of both realism *and* idealism, to be beyond cynicism but not as far as utopianism.

The Changing Values

The 'values' question in practitioner research has given rise to an historically specific series of answers. First there was the question of effectiveness - what works and what would work better? How can statutory obligations be fulfilled, how can needs be identified? There was a struggle for a comprehensive caring and compassionate service. Practitioners addressed their research to client needs, to counselling and to therapy. In brief, there was a medical model or 'metaphor-in-use' (Schon, 1984) for which the value was one of healing.

Next came intervention, client management and efficiency. Practices had heaped up and the economic climate was hostile to any suggestion of waste. Sometimes these values arose directly from practitioners' experiences, mostly they did not. A business model or metaphor-in-use gave forth the value of cost-saving. Practitioners who would be, or were, managers came to think of targets and strategies. They accepted that there had been waste, yet against this 'admission' there was the well-supported feeling that the need for the service was ever increasing.

The tension between development and defensiveness both created and partially concealed the emergence of 'advocacy'. In the absence of subsequent enabling legislation, 'equal opportunities' gave the only chance of overcoming sexism, racism and, by extension, poverty and disablement. A political metaphor has always been in use amongst practitioners. Some want to openly struggle for change, against prevailing social and economic forces. They speak of issues, marginality and exclusion. They question the insularity of the medical and business models and ask whose interests are being served by their use?

The Four As

There is an urgency in practitioner research, an urge to get a perspective or approach onto the policy agenda. The concerns have always been about quality, standards and performance indicators but rarely in those precise words. As the 1990s will be when quality-assurance, performance and value for money are 'high' on the agenda, social work by contact will become more a matter of social work by contract.

Thus 'operational leadership' is being added to 'organisational learning' (the epoch when social work in the statutory sector put its own house in order or resisted responding to apparent disarray). 'Operational leadership' is setting the standards for 'service delivery' by which contracts may be drawn up, continued or cancelled. Added then to *action plans, awareness programmes* and *advocacy* will be a practitioner research of *accountability* where social workers seek to establish criteria for a social work practice in which they are not directly involved. And because of this research, a fresh perspective will be taken on the acute cases with which they are directly involved as well as upon the direct responsibility for the most recent legislation.

The ideal of practitioner research is that during initial training social work trainees learn research by doing: through a critical, open-minded and fair test of practice and practical details. As seasoned practitioners they, at some point in their career, then research a segment of action, awareness, advocacy and accountability. This latter endeavour may be either 'in-house' or in partnership with an higher education provider. Thus for the benefit of themselves, the profession, the service and society they are making the links between the immediate action, the focus of delivery and organisation and the ever present balance between societal disease and social justice.

Good Faith

The reality principle in practitioner research is based upon the limited amount of time available being an accepted fact. The idealism is not in trying to perfect the design but to improve the accuracy of a search for significance. The question is not 'How much about all this can I say?' but 'What is most worth looking at and saying something about?'.

Refining the problem has therefore to be undertaken with confidentiality; contrasting good practice with malpractices, good experiences with bad ones. It is dangerous to rush this stage by grabbing hold of the first half - good idea to be expressed. The aim is to have a design that is less like a hammer and more like a key. Thus practitioner research pilots lines of enquiry almost from the outset. Enthusiasm rises but emotional entanglement is kept at a minimum - for the moment.

Most research works because subjects are helpful, long-suffering and eager to talk with somebody, as David Bowen insists. Practitioner research aims to reach beyond the obvious and orthodox exercise and towards the more dramatic discovery. This is a valid ambition. Practitioner-researchers want to discover something, or, more properly put, uncover the latent patterns which can enslave or enable professionals and clients alike. They want to see how much or how little has been achieved in the name of legislation. They want to find out where and how goals were redefined, provisions watered down, even victims created. Practitioners want to ask questions about 'us' in relation to 'them' and how sour relations can become more sweet. Practitioner-researchers want to reaffirm the 'good faith' which makes being a professional more than a middle class life style with a main line to human misery. They want to be able to say all these things and hear themselves saying them.

Part Two
State of the Art Studies

Placing People with Learning Difficulties in Employment from Adult Training Centres: The Search for Firm Evidence

TONY STOCKS

This stimulating narrative illustrates the extent of which broader social policy issues can be properly addressed from a modest starting point; here practical, training and skill acquisition issues. It also shows the extent to which practitioner-researchers are forced to be flexible in their work, adapting their research designs accordingly. Data availability and time constraint are always key factors.

The findings are significant. Widely reported and generally accepted figures on the placement of people with learning difficulties in open employment are almost certainly wrong. A study which began as an enquiry on how placements were achieved stripped away the illusions until it became a study of the opposite. Instead of leading to a good practice guide, the research led to explaining Attendance Day Centres' low achievement in terms of their low self-esteem and morale.

*A survey rarely gives rise to new special research methods. Rather surveys are a sustained and painstaking enquiry, which provide revealing insights during the data gathering process. Tony Stocks had the courage and tenacity to raise vital questions about the degree to which society fulfils its social responsibility to people with learning difficulties - **Editors**.*

Introduction

A primary function of Adult Training Centres is to prepare people with learning difficulties for open employment (ATC manager).

According to Whelan and Speake's survey of 1976, there were approximately 400 Adult Training Centres (ATCs) in England and Wales in 1973. Although research (Clarke and Hermelin, 1955; Gordon, Tizard and O'Connor, 1954; Tizard and Loos,

1954) had indicated that people with learning difficulties were capable of various types of industrial work, Whelan and Speake stated that, of the 24,252 trainees on ATC registers in February 1974, only 1,031 were said to have left the ATCs for open or sheltered employment. They estimated that the proportion of these placements that could be considered successful averaged about 4 per cent. If the primary function of ATCs was to prepare people with learning difficulties for open employment, this was clear evidence that the centres were not being very successful. The situation has various causes and consequences as I discovered from my research.

Research Beginnings
Identifying confusion/prejudice by employers towards people with learning difficulties

> *I will not employ them, having experience of employing two of them already. They were too aggressive and I had to give them the sack. They were from Grassfields Hospital.*

This statement was made by one of the employers who took part in this study. What he did not realise was that the hospital he had referred to was a psychiatric hospital for the mentally ill and that his two employees with learning difficulties were in fact mentally ill.

Staff qualifications and motivation
There is a large proportion of unqualified staff in ATCs\Social Education Centres (or SECs). Until 1964, there was no specific training for this work, apart from one pioneer course. About 170 people a year qualified for the Training Council's Diploma, about two-thirds of them being training centre staff seconded by local authorities. Since 1976 this course has been superseded by a two-year Certificate in Social Service, which, it was hoped, would improve the quality of training.

> *Who is going to employ this bloody lot with three million normal people out of a job?*

Throughout this report we shall find a deep vein of hopelessness among ATC managers and instructors.

Issues about the reliability, utility and consistency of assessment processes
Assessment represents a particularly crucial issue for trainees on work preparation courses in training centres. If an assessment is carried out, it must be relevant to the job in hand, but there are

different assessment schemes available each of which can be interpreted and applied in different ways.

Warnock (1978) recommended an assessment process involving five possible stages, each of which would require a wider range of expertise than the last. The Gunzberg Progress Assessment Chart is time-consuming and unwieldy, and often proves to be unreliable, different members of staff producing dissimilar results for the same trainee. Grant et al. (1973) compared ATC instructors' predictions of success and failure on specific tasks with individuals' actual performance, and found a high incidence of inaccurate prediction of failure.

In this research, every county visited was using different assessment forms, and in some counties ATC staff were designing and using their own methods of assessment. Only one of these new methods had been designed to match the individual trainee to a suitable job in open employment.

Knowledge about, access to, and utilisation of relevant research

Most of my staff are new and a bit green (ATC manager)

If trained staff are to be motivated to find suitable open employment for their trainees, they must not be denied access to this data, especially when the research is focusing on ways and means of employing people with learning difficulties. For example:

- The Habilitation Technology Project, run by Whelan from 1977-1983 at the Hester Adrian Research Centre, is aimed at developing learning packages such as Copewell[1] for use with the people with learning difficulties in adult training centres.
- Kierman, of the Thomas Coram Research Unit, has completed a project on the use of sign language with people with learning difficulties.
- A project carried out by Poon at King's College Department of Electronic and Electrical Engineering intends to speed up communication between people with learning difficulties using a micro processor based aid.
- Travers, at Exeter University School of Education, has examined the effects of physical education and sport in schools and adult centres for people with learning difficulties.

There are questions, then, about what research is available, what can be practically applied; and what is most useful; and, not least of all, who has all this information in the field?

My Proposed Research

My own experience in ATCs prompted an investigation of those circumstances in which open employment placements are successfully made. During a Certificate of Social Service (CSS) course I experimented with a novel method of assessment based on the repertory grid technique and on my return to the ATC in which I worked, I was able to implement an open employment project. This experience convinced me that open placements were possible. So I decided to carry out a survey of placements in a number of local authorities, with a view to identifying the factors that might serve to underpin a successful open employment programme.

The original design

My research was to be a retrospective and comparative analysis of the conditions and circumstances surrounding the placement in open employment of trainees from adult training centres. My aim was to analyse conditions and circumstances surrounding placements with a view to determining the significant factors responsible for relative success or relative lack of success, while remaining sensitive to the unanticipated influences. In summary, my study was originally designed to identify proven models of practice in ATCs, thereby increasing trainee throughput, and reduce the waste of both physical and human resources.

The research implied a number of different sources of data: interviews with main actors: trainees, families, ATC staff, employers, work colleagues, professionals, others and documentary analysis of case records and file. Findings were also to be made available to all participating authorities. As it turned out, this original design proved unworkable and for reasons that will become clear, this required a change of gear, and a shift in research aims. But let me first explain my original research sampling frame before explaining why I had to abandon it.

Establishing the original sampling frame

Fifteen local authorities in the south east of England were asked to participate in the survey. Eight agreed, four refused and three did not reply to the letters. Two of the eight local authorities who agreed to the survey were used in pilot work.

The six remaining local authorities in this research project provided a total sample of 39 ATCs/SECs, with a trainee/student population of 4,302. Based on Whelan and Speake's figures one might have anticipated, given this population, that placements into open employment would number between 80 and 150, and maybe slightly lower (to account for rises in overall levels of unemployment) during the course of a year. A sufficiently large sample of trainees for the project was confidently expected.

A postal questionnaire, similar in design to that used by Whelan and Speake, was circulated to all the 39 ATC/SECs. Copies of the postal questionnaires were also sent to the Social Service Directors and Assistant Directors of Planning and Research for their information. It requested basic information on those trainees who, during the survey period (12 months, from 31 March 1981 to 1 April 1982) had been placed in open employment, irrespective of whether they had returned to the ATC during the same period. Questionnaires returned (n=39), showed that out of this 4,302 figure the number of trainees leaving these establishments for open employment was just 25, an overall average placement percentage of 0.58.

Once the 39 questionnaires had been returned, it proved necessary through telephone calls and personal visits to check the reliability of information supplied. For example two trainees were alleged to have been placed into open employment by a social worker but a telephone conversation with their ATC manager revealed that the trainees had been placed in a college, and were attending a course. Not only was this not a case of open employment, it was not even a case of sheltered employment. Further explanations revealed that eight of the original twenty five trainees were placed outside the survey period. By December 1981, there were seventeen 'live' cases, an overall percentage of 0.4 who had left for open employment during the survey period.

The Revised Research Project (1)

The aims of the research project were now revised. A reasonable conclusion was that it is now more difficult, for various reasons, to place trainees in open employment, and the key question now was: given that it *is* more difficult, how is it achieved at all? What methods and techniques are being used to identify even this modest number of placements, and under what conditions are placements successfully realised? In other words, the research was no longer conceived as a contrast between relatively successful and relatively unsuccessful placements. Instead, it was to be a set of case studies.

It was initially planned to begin my interviews with ATC staff, employers, key workers, employees, the trainee's parents/ guardians, trainees, and various professional workers. Appointments with ATC managers were the first to be arranged. If I had expected to establish a simple and reliable system of appointments made, followed by interviews conducted, I was soon disillusioned. Appointments were regularly broken, and interviews had to be re-arranged, or fitted in to some other part of the research schedule. Turning up for one pre-arranged appointment with an ATC manager, I discovered that no-one at the centre knew where he was. After waiting for over two hours, I decided that, rather than waste the whole day, I would visit the trainee's employer instead. With fieldwork time beginning to run out, I stopped making appointments, and just turned up the ATCs/SECs. Having identified myself, I would ask to see the manager and was invariably given an immediate interview. 'Why didn't you make an appointment? We've nothing to hide', was a typical remark before, and sometimes after the interview. I apologised, but said nothing of previous experiences when using the appointments system.

Further sample shrinkage

A detailed re-examination of all 17 cases was undertaken. I revisited all the ATC/SECs concerned, interviewed staff, trainees, parents, employers, employees and social workers, in order to gain as much detailed information as possible about the circumstances surrounding the placements. This was a far from easy task and it soon transpired that the total sample was even smaller than the apparent figure of 17. The final breakdown of cases and placements is produced in Table I.

Summary of the revised research project

The position can be summarised by saying that in six local authorities, 39 ATC/SECs, and a total trainee population of 4,302, I discovered only *one new case* of the type I was seeking i.e. open employment placements made by ATC/SECs within the specified period.

Although this unexpected, and rather depressing, situation can partly be accounted for by pointing to the unsystematic nature of ATC/SEC records, it is difficult to avoid the conclusion that some of the inaccurate information supplied by the postal questionnaire was known to be inaccurate by those who supplied it. Nevertheless, they continued to insist on its accuracy, even when I made direct personal contact with them, and even when they were aware that I would be checking the facts for myself. This raises the perennial but important question about the reliability of statistics collected on a postal return basis. It also raises questions about the validity of the estimates (Whelan and Speake, 1976) which this research project took as a starting point.

Table 1
A Breakdown of Non-Genuine and Genuine Cases of Trainee Placement in Open Employment During The One Year Specified Period (i)

Non-genuine cases	
Open employment placements outside the specified period	6
Entry to further education outside the specified period	4
Entry to further education during the specified period	1
Initiation of work experience during the specified period	1
Placement in sheltered employment	1
Sub-Total	**13**
Arguably genuine cases	
Placed by the ATC/SEC (Note iii)	2
Placed by hostel warden (Note iv)	1
Returned to former employment, following the rebuilding of a laundry destroyed by fire (Note ii)	2
Sub-total	**5**
Total	**18**

i.   *An additional, eighteenth, case was discovered, almost by accident, during a search of ATC/SEC records.*
ii. *The two trainees returning to the laundry had originally begun employment there some ten years previously. They had returned to the ATC while the laundry was being rebuilt following a fire.*
iii. *These cases, in which the ATC itself was responsible for the placement, includes one known to me, on the research course organised prior to me taking up my position on the research course at Cranfield.*
iv. *Of these three genuine cases placed, either by the ATC/SEC or by a hostel warden, two returned to the SECs within three months. The third, who is still employed, is the trainee already known to me and referred to in note (iii).*

The Revised Research Project (2)

It appeared that open employment placements hardly existed at all, and the obvious question was - why?

Two main reasons suggested themselves, through discussion with ATC staff: first, the difficulty of matching trainees to jobs; second, the unemployment situation. Three further elements were therefore introduced into the research. In the first place, I decided to interview ATC managers who had not even claimed that they had made open employment placements, and ask them why they had been unable to do so. Second, I gave myself an opportunity to experiment further with the method of assessment and matching which I had observed during my CSS course. Third, I determined to undertake a survey of potential employers, in at least one town or city, to discover whether there really were no jobs available that people with learning difficulties could do.

The research project was now revised again and finally consisted of 18 case studies, describing the circumstances surrounding each apparent 'placement' (both non-genuine and genuine cases) in some detail, and commenting on the unduly investigative nature of the work required to unearth them; interviews with ATC/SEC staff seeking their views on the reasons why open employment placements are not being made; interviews with employers, to discover whether their views of feasibility of placements coincided with the view of ATC/SEC staff; and further experiments with my own method of assessment and preparation in the one genuine case which was already known. Despite this sharp change of direction the research project still produced a range of valid findings, and these are summarised below.

Summary of the study's main findings

1. From 39 ATCs, and a total trainee population of 4,302, I discovered five successful cases within the survey period of one year, only two of which were genuine direct placements.

2. Of the five successful cases, in only one could it be said that there was a 'method' of placement. For the rest, procedures are ad hoc, unsystematic, and not particularly well thought out. There is no planning to speak of, little contact of any kind between suitable employers and ATCs and no training of prospective employees, either at the ATC or on site.

3. Critically, reliable information about ATCs trainees is particularly difficult to obtain. This is partly explained by inadequate records, but there remains the suspicion that some of those who offered information were aware that it was, to some degree or another, inaccurate. It is also clear that many ATCs do not keep themselves informed of developments once a trainee leaves the centre, whether for open employment, further education, or any other reason. In many instances, information about what happens *inside* the ATC is unreliable. Wall charts, programmes and timetables do not necessarily reflect how the majority of trainees actually spend their time.

4. The staple diet of ATCs is still contract work. It is an ironic fact that the trainees in 'social education centres' spent more time on contract work than those in 'adult training centres'. In either case, there is little that could accurately be called 'training' or 'education' going on.

5. According to ATC staff the reasons why ATCs do not make open employment placements vary. They include: staff shortages; inadequately trained staff; lightweight Social

Services management; complicated and time-consuming methods of assessment. The most popular explanation, however, was 'unemployment'. This argument may not be as strong as it looks. A study of 20 employers, located near two ATCs, unearthed 15 jobs which were considered (by myself and the employers) suitable for mentally handicapped people. These jobs carry wages in the 'poverty trap' range (£40-£75 approximately). Some jobs therefore do exist, and could be made available to people with learning difficulties. The questions remain: *should* these sorts of low paid jobs be the only ones offered to the majority of people with learning difficulties? and second what view does the trainee have of such jobs?

6. Although not detailed here it seemed, in the 'employer study' that, in principle, employers are willing to employ people with learning difficulties, and can be enthusiastic about this prospect. In particular, when conditions are attached to trainee employment and support is given by ATCs for trainees in employment, employers were more committed and reassured. This 'system of placement' included a method of identifying suitable work environments for individual trainees, based on Kelly's Repertory Grid. Besides specifying the kind of work environment that might suit individuals, it also indicated cases in which it might be better advised not to try and place the trainee in a job outside the centre.

Conclusions: Simply a Question of Staff Reorganisation and Retraining?

One of the functions of ATCs has always been to make open employment placements - to find suitable jobs, and train people with learning difficulties for them. The question arises: how seriously are we to take this function given the above findings that, at most; 0.58 per cent of trainees were found open employment in the one year research period. There are two principle options.

The positive option

On the basis of this study, it is possible to argue that it is feasible to make open employment placements. One can imagine how it might be organised: 'Work placement' officers, attached to a group of ATCs, could be appointed. It is unrealistic to expect the majority of ATC instructors to be involved in this kind of work, given their supervisory responsibilities.

First it would be their task, to find suitable jobs, undeterred by the apparently 'common sense' knowledge that they do not exist.

Second they would assess prospective recruits from the centres by some reliable, but uncomplicated, method.

Third having matched trainees to vacancies, they would carry out a job analysis, and organise appropriate training for the individuals concerned.

Fourth they would negotiate the conditions of employment with the employer.

Fifth they would monitor the placement regularly once it had begun.

One could not expect to place too many trainees in a year. But at least two or three per authority, done in this systematic way, would be an improvement on the current state of affairs. The effect on the climate of opinion, and on the morale, in ATCs might be even more significant, in the long run, than the number of his successes. The prevailing moods in the ATCs (and SECs) are those of resignation, pessimism and despair and a more out-going, ultimately more confident, approach to work placement might just help to reverse or stem these negative attitudes. Also, at a macro level, existing legislation concerning the statutory employment of people with learning difficulties needs strengthening, and better enforcing.

The negative option

This option is more depressing: to yield to the claim that making placements, even if jobs can be found, is not worth the effort. What need of work when your 'business' is 'social education'? This would be more convincing (perhaps!) if the change of name were accompanied by a change of regime and a change of orientation. But, in this study I have already noted the irony that supervision of contract work (with staff frequently helping to maintain quotas) was even more rife in the SECs than in the ATCs. If we strip away the rhetoric and pretension, we are left with something painfully recognisable: a system of social control in the form of containment and exploitation. One is reminded of prisoners sewing mailbags.

Conclusion

If ATCs are places of supervision and containment, then it may be better to acknowledge that than to try and conceal it even from ourselves. The move towards 'social education' *may* signal a transition towards some systematic form of caring and positive day care for people with learning difficulties. What cannot be allowed is a continuation of the current position, in which the apparent function of work training, conceals a system which is supposed to have become extinct 50 or 100 years ago. The new 'workhouses' may be a somewhat exaggerated and unpleasant description of modern ATC/SECs, but its very pungency may prompt us into thinking about the similarities and, even better, into trying to do something to improve them, as in the above positive option.

Footnotes

1. In this study, only two of the managers mentioned Copewell and even they had only just received it.

The Search for Emergency Social Service Duty Systems

BERNARD C. WEBB

Usually the problem is sufficiently complex and interesting to warrant the collection of different types of data, from different sources, and in different forms. This piece, illustrates the ingenuity, energy and breadth of vision needed to tackle the problem in hand. At the heart of a survey is its sampling frame. This study shows the usefulness of a telephone survey in tracking down respondents. Are emergency social service duty systems, an alert owl, a bat awaiting nightfall, or a mole making occasional outings but rarely seen by others?

*As may be becoming apparent from reading Tony Stock's article earlier, the more systems are closed and managed through elaborate codes the less they may be doing. There are devices which prevent close inspection, devices which even 'professionals-in-the-know' may find daunting. How much more difficult must the codes be for clients panicked by the pressure of need? - **Editors.***

Making the Research List

By telephoning each emergency number in the evening I was able to determine out-of-hours arrangements in 118 of the 131 Social Service Departments in the United Kingdom. I began by taking a sample of departments on the basis of whether they operated a standby system, a specialist team, or had no service at all. The sampling frame I used was my Social Service Department's list of other department's emergency telephone numbers. After carrying out a pilot study, I discovered that the list was not accurate, probably due to the fairly frequent changes which are typical of departments in this area, and to the lack of understanding of the system's operation on the part of some answering services, often residential units. Sixteen of the 118 departments were unwilling to provide the information, so I telephoned their Headquarters the following morning and asked to speak to the Directors. Only three people gave me the information I needed.[1] The others either refused, or suggested I write to the Director, with no guarantee that my letter would be answered, or to the Association of Directors of Social Services. I now re-numbered the departments in the initial categories and, using random numbers, selected 12 specialist teams (from 58), nine standby systems (from 48), and three with no service (from 15, 14 of them having disputes going on, while the other had no service as policy, and I specifically included this one). I also chose two from the remaining 13 and found that one had a specialist team and the other a standby system. The sample was about 20 per cent of the total. I selected two from each category as reserves. I planned to contact Directors of the departments with no service to find out why they had none, whether there were arrangements for contact if necessary, and what consequences the lack of service had produced. I then contacted the police as major referrers to Social Services Department out-of-hours systems.

One such contact is worth recording here. I telephoned the emergency number, later confirming it in the *Social Services Yearbook 1981,* and found it to be a hospital switchboard. The receptionist told me it was the wrong number and she thought the Social Services closed at 17.00. I then checked with the police, as a major 24 hour emergency service, and an important referrer to Social Services out-of-hours systems. A Sergeant told me he also thought the department closed at 17.00 and that if he or his colleagues were faced with a 'social problem' they would deal with it as best they could and would use the NSPCC if necessary when children were involved. The following morning I telephoned the department's headquarters and spoke to an Assistant Director who was extremely abrupt, and told me in a not particularly helpful way that he would consider giving me the information if I wrote to him. When I mentioned the problem I had encountered in attempting to contact the emergency duty social worker, he told me it was none of my business, despite my pointing out that the number was listed officially and that it is often necessary for out-of-hours staff in different departments to contact each other about people, for instance, children who have run away from children's homes in their respective areas, and that while it can be inconvenient if they are unable to make contact it can also be disastrous, particularly for clients. I later discovered that this department actually operated a standby system at this time, but that staff on the rota were only carrying out the work reluctantly.

Devising the Questions

For comparative purposes I decided to interview three or four people, on standby in each department and, because they are much fewer, two in each specialist team. I divided the interviews into two parts, one to obtain information about the particular system, and the other to discover how the duty officer would respond to certain referrals. The first part consisted of the following questions, which were designed to show how the system actually operated, what staff and resources were used, and how committed to the job were the duty officers.

1. Does your department have a standby rota of day-time staff or a specialist team?
2. How many people are involved and how often are they on duty?
3. Are all the staff qualified, and what experience do they have?
4. What training is given?
5. What professional/advisory 'back-up' in terms of senior staff for consultation and others for escort duty, is available?
6. What resources are provided, for instance telephone numbers of useful agencies, and places in residential units?
7. Is it possible to keep records and store information about potential emergencies? If not has this caused any problems?
8. Is the system monitored to show the number and content of calls and action taken?
9. What sort of area is covered?
10. Is it possible to check the non-accidental injury register?
11. How is contact made with the service?
12. Do you feel your department has an obligation to provide an emergency service? How do you feel about being involved in providing it?

In the second part 'real situations' were described to duty officers, and they were asked how they would respond. All were actual referrals which I had dealt with while on out-of-hours duty. I include example 3. as an illustration of the sorts of problems that are faced by emergency duty workers.

1. A call is received from someone who is distressed, somewhat irrational, and unable to explain the problem or give any background information except (a) she has the care of a young child; (b) he is a single person with no children. Depending on the response a follow-up question may be asked: 'Would you consider a compulsory admission under the Mental Health Act'?
2. A call is received from a distraught parent claiming to be having problems with a child who is out of control, steals from home, and hits the younger children. She threatens to abandon them if the child is not removed.
3. You are contacted by a children's home where parents of a child resident there by order of a Court/Children's Hearing, are insisting that the child be returned to them immediately.

A follow-up question would be: 'Suppose the parents allege ill-treatment of the child by staff?'

Gaining Access

My next worry was how to gain access to duty officers. I decided the simplest way was to contact the duty officers by telephoning their department's emergency number out-of-hours and asking if they would be willing to take part in the study, after describing it to them briefly. Most were immediately willing to do so, while others preferred to think about it for a day or two. Five people, in three areas, were willing to give information about their department's service but not to take part in the rest of the study. Three specialist teams and two standby systems were ruled out because staff were unwilling to co-operate, and the reserves therefore had to be used. The main reasons for refusal seemed to be that their department would not allow it or that they were too busy. Four specialist teams, and five standby systems operated a call-back system whereby the referrer telephones the emergency number and speaks to someone who is not a social worker and not necessarily an employee of a Social Services Department. This person takes the caller's telephone number and passes it to the duty officer who then telephones to discuss the problem. A majority of the duty officers in these areas seemed to be over-cautious when they called me back, sometimes to the point of appearing unhelpful, probably because they were unaware of the sort of problem that would be facing them.

Once staff had agreed to participate, I arranged to interview them either over the telephone in our own time, or in a face-to-face meeting, again in our own time, depending on the areas accessibility to me. Telephone interviews made up about 65 per cent of the study. In the pilot I found it easier to keep to the actual questions to be asked - rather than leading the respondent when interviewing by telephone. Self-discipline was more difficult face-to-face. However, having recognised this difficulty, I was better able to overcome it in the main study. Duty officers in specialist teams seemed to be more confident over the telephone than those in standby systems and appeared to be more able to take time to consider their answers.

I also interviewed 12 clients who have used the service - some in an area with a specialist team, and others in an area with a standby system - and discussed with day-time workers (in the former area) their attitude towards their department's specialist team. I also contacted the police, (mainly sergeants and constables) in areas selected, as a major referrer, to determine why they do or do not use the service and what response they receive. Finally I concentrated on one area with a specialist team, to consider all referrals over two periods (each of one month's duration a year apart) to look at numbers of referrals, their content and the team's response. I had planned to carry out the same process in an area with a standby system but was unable to find a suitably similar department which would cooperate.

Of the two departments I contacted one already had what its Director felt was the optimum number of external projects being carried out, while the other department's Director did not feel that the carrying out of any research in his department at that time would be 'conducive to good staff morale'.

I feel that when all of these different parts of the study were taken together, I obtained an overall picture of the types of system currently in use, showing how they are staffed and how they operate, paying particular attention to the way duty officers actually respond when contacted, and emphasising strengths and weaknesses in the systems and how innovations to improve practice may be introduced.

Black and White Day-Centres

GRACE THOMAS

Surveys, 'state of the art' enquiries, vary in scale and subject matter. There can be studies of national provisions, regional matters and local conditions. The subject matter is often about the identity of participants but in practitioner research the issues of participation also feature strongly too.

Grace Thomas surveyed Day Centres in Oxford city and learnt about the problems they face. Her survey began with seven centres and then refined its enquiries to two. She found that Day Centres were virtually segregated into those for blacks and those for whites. In this way there is first a 'broad-mesh' survey of the similarities in Day Centres, then a finer mesh survey of differences leading to an in-depth survey.

*Another way of expressing Grace Thomas's approach is that of a narrowing funnel in which the problem tapers first from democratic control to economic insecurity, and then tapers further to a problem of an embedded, taken for granted racism - **Editors.***

Common Criticisms
The structure of management

Two co-ordinators, one from a day-centre for white clients, and the other from a black establishment mentioned that the structure of the management of their centres was detrimental to any meaningful development. These allegations were supported by many of the clients interviewed at these centres. The complaints were:

* There are too many people on the board of governors and the executive committees.
* That often individual members on these decision-making bodies become too powerful and dictatorial, thus often only a few people control decision-making. The consequences of this situation are that policies are undemocratic and narrow and often dogmatic. It is argued that those who suffer are the staff who have to implement such policies, and the clients who have to put up with the realities of such policies.

At the Roots Day Centre clients were scathing about what they considered to be an unusually large executive which did very little to advance the cause of the clients.

But in all the centres there were also arguments for such large numbers on the board of governors and the executive committees. A large number meant ensuring representation of all interest groups. Unfortunately the argument about powerful and dictatorial individuals who dominate such bodies, offsets the idea of fair representation. Large numbers also tend to encourage unnecessary bureaucracy. A question is therefore raised as to how best a balanced and democratic representation can be achieved in the management structure of these Day Centres?

Many of the Day Centres examined elect clients to their decision-making panels. This was more so in the Afro-Caribbean Day Centres. But in all the Day Centres studied, except the Caribbean Centre and the Barton Lunch Club, there were bitter complaints about the clients' views not being taken seriously by those who were responsible for the major decision-making. At the UB40, the situation has demoralised the clients because those I spoke to claim that clients are never consulted before any decision is taken.

Although the Roots' clients play an active role in decision-making, those interviewed argued that their views were usually ignored. They also complained that they were often not consulted before decisions were made. Obviously this is a controversial situation. It may be easy to ignore these clients, especially the young unemployed. But that may be detrimental if these centres wish to make any meaningful changes. I was very surprised by the level of intelligence and the articulate manner in which those I interviewed expressed their views about the issues that affect them. They are able to talk about their plight so intelligently, and are fully aware of their situation. They have their hopes and fears, and unlike those who are better off socio-economically, the majority of them seemed sensitive about each others plight.

Funding: the major problem which affects the infrastructure of the centres

Of the seven Day Centres in Oxford City only two were fully sponsored and managed by the Social Services. These two centres were Merlin Road Mothers' and Children's Group, and the Blackbird Leys Mothers' and Children's Group. Both co-ordinators said that they also raise funds by other means. But their main financial support can be traced to the Social Services. The historical establishment of the five other centres can be traced back to either self-help groups in the case of all the Afro-Caribbean Day Centres and the Barton Old People's Lunch Club.

The observation made during this study is the difficult nature under which the majority of these Day Centres operate. The most difficult problems which the organisers have to face are finding sufficient finance to keep the centres going. Lack of adequate funding of these centres means poor quality of services for clients. It also means a lot of anxiety for staff. Uncertainties as to whether a centre would be funded on a short term basis creates demoralisation. I dare not talk about long term funding, because only two out of the seven centres enjoy any long term funding.

The Merlin Road Mothers' and Children's Group is a special Social Services project. It is therefore unlikely to be starved of funds. On the other hand, the Blackbird Leys Mothers' and Children's Group, although a Social Services project, has not got the label of a special case. Thus its system of funding is poor and irregular. The children do not even have proper chairs and tables and are forced to make do with huge church tables and chairs which are totally inappropriate for toddlers, and the premises used by this group are inadequate. In fact, compared with the Merlin Road, children at the Blackbird Leys' Neighbourhood Centre Nursery are at a disadvantage in practically every aspect. It seems hardly just or fair to treat children whose socio-economic backgrounds are almost similar in such different ways. It is necessary that the disadvantage gap between the two centres must be closed by the Social Services to give them the credibility and fairness.

Justice and credibility aside, if the Social Services are unable to update other nurseries they are in charge of to a decent standard, there is no doubt that they would be faced with many more troubles like Merlin Road. In this case, the saying 'A stitch in time saves nine' surely applies.

The Barton Old People's Lunch Club is self-financing. They raise the bulk of their funds through raffles, bingo, personal contributions and jumble sales. They seemed contented about most of the services they have created for themselves. However, the majority of the respondents went straight to the point about the things that they felt discontented with. They made it clear that they have contributed their lifetime's best during the war and after, to build the economy of this society. At retirement they feel that the least the state can do for them is the reward of a modern entertainment hall with suitable amenities. Particularly, many of them felt strongly about the poor and unsuitable toilet facilities they have to put up with. Some suggested that the authorities need to consider putting up a brand new hall with suitable entertainment and toilet amenities for them. Although the Social Services subsidise the food given to these old people on Wednesdays, it is clear that the bulk of funding falls onto the members. It therefore seems only fair that this group's request must be seriously considered. Unsuitable toilet amenities are a danger to the old and often frail people who need every support they can hold on to.

I was told about the agony which staff have been through in getting funding for the UB40, I viewed the situation with more than just academic interest. I felt the difficulties to obtain funding had created unnecessary panic and tension among staff and clients alike. After all, the UB40 as one of the staff put it is the authority's own 'garbage pit'. If that is so, then one may ask why it is necessary to make funding difficult for such a project? There is no doubt that the idea of creating projects like that for the unemployed is a bright idea. But the scope they give to the youngsters seems too narrow. There is a need to introduce skills like plastering, bricklaying, serious carpentry, painting and decorating, as well as practical botany, sewing and knitting, art, and especially the creating of clothes' patterns should be included in the projects. This practical training would be more appropriate and realistic for the long term unemployed. Many more full time specialist trainers should be employed in addition to those they have already.

Is There a Difference in Pattern of Use?
Yes, there are differences among black and white clients in their way of Day Centre use. The most significant difference is that among the Afro-Caribbeans both young and older generations have practically no previous experience of Day Centres. The white clients, on the other hand, have extensive experience of Day Centres, and most use more than two Day Centres at the time of this study. These patterns are clearly illustrated below.

Referrals and Rate of Attendance
Only two of the seven centres studied had any consistent system of statutory referrals. These were the Blackbird Leys and the Merlin Road Mothers' and Children's Groups. At these two centres referrals were by social workers and health visitors.

The remaining five centres did not seem to have any statutory referrals at all. Instead, respondents claimed they either were recommended to use the centres by friends, relatives, or had done so on their own initiative. This was surprising because although only the first two centres were completely sponsored by the Social Services, there was not a single one of the remaining centres which the Social Services were not concerned with in one way or another. Yet they did not seem to have included these centres in their network of provision available to their clients.

The rate of attendance in most centres seemed to be fairly good. But the Afro-Caribbean Day Centres for the elderly, and the mothers' and children's groups seemed to be poorly attended. The reasons given by the staff were seasonal fluctuations and lack of confidence among many black people to attend Day Centres.

Day Centre Use

The Afro-Caribbeans claimed that they were not welcomed by the white indigenous Day Centre users. Their evidence was revealed in the form of personal experiences of racial attacks, fighting, insults, and taunting at conventional Day Centres. They said this treatment was the basis of their fear and the objections they had about attending conventional Day Centres.

There were clear indications that the Afro-Caribbean respondents felt the Social Services did not make provision for their cultural needs at the conventional Day Centres. Other allegations were that the black youths who braved the storm to attend the conventional Day Centres were fortunate to escape physical attacks and racial insults yet were ignored at these centres by both staff and clients. This point was particularly stressed by an Afro-Caribbean visitor from the United States, and was substantiated by other respondents. Other respondents mentioned that they consequently felt inhibited and could not 'be themselves' at conventional Day Centres.

Attention was then directed at the conventional Day Centres to find out whether the allegations made by the black respondents were true or false. At the pre-dominantly white youth unemployed Day Centre, the UB40, half of the respondents claimed they were not racists, and that they would not mind sharing their facilities with clients from different cultural backgrounds. The other half of the respondents admitted that their own parents were racists. They themselves have not been taught how to cope with a multi-racial society. But none of them admitted that they were racists who would oppose the use of their centre by youth from different cultural backgrounds.

The enquiry was taken a step further. I interviewed the co-ordinator, the staff, and the ex-clients. The intention was to find out the truth about racism at the UB40, and how it prevents others from using the facilities there. There was confirmation that there were actually racist gangs at the UB40 who do not countenance the use of the centre by people from other culture. These groups are not only a problem for black people who wish to use the centre, they are also a bad influence on the young unemployed, and a menace to the staff. Though the staff had, in the past, done their best to get rid of such people, they have not got enough power or official backing to do so. Ironically, the disruptive activities of these people has, in the past, invited threats from the authorities to close the place down. The question which this point raises is who was responsible for taking action against such a group? Was it the authorities, or the staff who had very little power?

The other allegations of the Afro-Caribbean respondents were also substantiated at the UB40. All the staff and the volunteers were white. Furthermore there were no indications that provisions of any kind had been made for people of different cultural backgrounds. But there was one important issue which I could not in all honesty say I noted. The staff did not show any signs of being racists. On the contrary I found them friendly, sincere and co-operative. I was only a black research student. So would the situation have been different if I had gone there as a client?

The investigations of the experience and the use of Day Centres among the Afro-Caribbean elderly was still more depressing. In fact, the situation of the elderly black was worse than I had imagined. The respondents claimed that their past experience of racism, insults and racial attacks deterred them from using any conventional Day Centres. One elderly woman thought such Day Centres were created solely for white people. She had never thought black people could go near such places. And even if they could she would never dare to venture into white people's Day Centres because of her past experience of racism.

The chairman of the Caribbean Centre who started the group expressed his endless frustration about trying to persuade the black elderly to join. He stated that the majority of black elderly are still afraid to venture out and make use of Social Services provisions. They tended to associate such services with their past experience of racism and discrimination. It would, therefore, take years of persuasion to convince them to use such services.

To find out whether or not the black elderly make use of the conventional Day Centres, enquiries were made at the matching conventional elderly Day Centre at Barton. There had in the past been a couple of black people - Indians, I was told. But there were controversial reasons why these clients left the club and never came back. Some respondents suggested they were hurt by racist remarks some one made. But I was unable to get the true story. However the majority of the respondents claimed they 'would not mind' elderly people from other cultures using their centre. But two people did not like the idea of black people sharing their amenities.

Enquiries at the two Afro-Caribbean established nurseries to find out about use and experience of the conventional nurseries proved almost as negative. The majority of the black parents at the Roots Nursery, and the Blackbird Leys did not use the conventional nurseries. There were widespread allegations and fear about black children being treated badly at the conventional Day Centres. The social worker who started the Blackbird Leys mothers' and children's group confirmed that before the advent of that group, most of the black single parents did not use any nurseries. They were stuck at home with their children owing to fear of racism at the conventional nurseries.

What was significant was that enquiries at the matching conventional Day Centre showed that not many black children were referred to use the Merlin Road Nursery which was supposed to be a special centre for children at risk.

Is There a Difference in the Quality of Services Provided?

Again the answer is definitely yes. There were great differences between the quality of services for the conventional Day Centres and the black established ones. Although black and white Day Centre users tend to come mainly from the poor of society, it seemed clear that the blacks are the poorest of the poor, and the sort of provisions given them reflect this in all centres.

The contrast between the two nurseries for black children and the Merlin Road which was for dominantly white children was so great. The nurseries for black children were poorly equipped. Both nurseries for black children had no trained nursery teachers and funding was scanty and erratic. Merlin Road on the other hand, was well funded, well equipped, have trained staff and the premises they use are ideal. Like the other conventional Day Centres mentioned the staff were all white. Throughout the time of this study at the place, there was no sign that they made any provision in terms of food and recreational facilities for children from other cultures.

These disparities in the provision of nursery facilities for the dominantly black groups is very serious indeed. Juliet Cheetham has written about the disproportionate rates of reception into care of black children. (Cheetham, 1984, p.5; also Gordon and Newnham, 1986, p.24).

Clearly, if black children are disadvantaged right from the beginning of their education at the nursery, then a very serious retardation problem lies ahead. It is true that many complicated problems contribute to the disproportionate rates of black children in care. But it could also be said that poor educational achievement by black children can be a contributory factor to several problems including being taken into care. A disappointed and frustrated mother can be forced into acting irrationally.

Both Blackbird Leys and Merlin Road were directly under the Social Services. The mothers of the infants at these nurseries had similar socio-economic problems. It did not make sense for the Social Services to make a special case out of one group and leave the other group at a disadvantage. Otherwise a question may be asked: Was it because the Blackbird Leys Nursery catered for mainly black children that they had been left with the poorest provisions? Or, most strongly, had the Social Services failed the black community?

A comparison of the quality of services for youth Day Centres showed that one cannot say that the UB40 clients were socio-economically any better off than their Roots counter parts. But they certainly had much better facilities in terms of organised projects which the Roots did not have. Although the Social Services were not directly involved with the running of the place, they were actively involved with drug advice and helping with accommodation problems. They had practically no involvement at the Roots Day Centre - except with individual clients who needed special attention and a bit of interest in the nursery.

The elderly Afro-Caribbeans regard the quality of services they got as poor. The only thing they had no complaints about was the organisation of their centre which was done by one of them. The premises they were using was borrowed. They were unable to use it as many times as they wanted. They had no storage cupboards. Furthermore they were limited to one room, because of the difficulties of climbing the stairs and the toilet facilities were said to be poor.

This was in contrast with the Barton's Old People's Lunch Club where the structure of the premises was suitable for the aged. There were no stairs, they had storage facilities and enough room to move about (although the Barton old people also complained about poor toilet facilities).

Why Was There a Gap Between the Two?

The black Day Centre clients interviewed attributed the gap between the two groups on all the issues discussed to racism and discrimination. For example, on the issue of Day Centre provisions they pointed out that the failure to make provision for the cultural needs of the minority ethnic groups suggests that the social service itself was the culprit of discrimination. If the services were for all citizens regardless of colour, then such services must reflect the diverse cultural interests of the members of the society. Providing for the majority cultural group alone amounts to discrimination.

Another important complaint, according to them, was the virtual absence of black staff members at the Social Services and the various Day Centres. At the time of this research there was only one black social worker in the social service department. There was not a single black employee in any significant position at the conventional Day Centres. The black respondents pointed out that the exclusion of black people from responsible positions in the Social Services make them suspicious of the whole system. They say it is an effective way of rejecting blacks. Without blacks in responsible positions, they do not see how their interests could be fairly represented.

The most significant finding of the study is the fact that the Social Services has not been able to do anything about the fundamental problem which made it impossible for the minority ethnic groups to use the conventional Day Centres - racism. This situation was said to be the major reason why the Afro-Caribbeans decided to establish separate Day Centres for members of their community who needed them.

The findings of this study show that the gap between black and white go deeper than the mere provision of Day Centre services. Racism affects practically every aspect of the lives of the majority of Afro-Caribbeans. This allegation was substantiated by the revelations of the personal experiences of the black respondents. There are clear indications that discriminatory provision of services affects the life of the black infant at the nursery owing to the poor Social Services' provisions for the predominantly black people's centres. The stories of the black respondents show that the educational disadvantage continues through school often by the activities of white teachers who are racist. This racism which most black children claim that they suffer tends to reduce their chances of educational success, and often gives them very little room to progress socio-economically. The majority of the black youth unemployed blame their problems on racism in this society.

Racism does not only affect Afro-Caribbean youths. Right from the beginning of their migration to this country the Afro-Caribbean elderly respondents claim life has been a nightmare. Racism affected them at work, in the streets, in health care, and in their efforts to get accommodation. In other words, racism penetrated into their domestic affairs. So there was no relief anywhere.

Surprisingly, one of the most significant observations made in this study is the fact that the majority of the white respondents were totally unaware, and some undisturbed, about racism. Some of these white respondents seemed so sheltered that racism did not seem to intrude on any aspect of their lives. Yet others made it clear that racism was not part of their problems. They said they were not black, and racism is the problem of the black people.

Coping with racism is a crucial element in the life of many black respondents of this study. I was told that it is essential to devise coping strategies to enable life to go on, to protect self, family and friends, as well as property. Coping strategies as were revealed to me, are essential in most black people's life in Britain, to ensure personal and psychological stability. During this study I discovered that the older Afro-Caribbean elderly adopted different coping strategies to that of the younger generations. The older generations advocated patience and ignoring racism to enable them to get on with their work and their lives. Many of the respondents admitted that this softly, softly approach to racism hurt them in many ways. But some argued that at least they were able to stay in work longer. They managed to put up with the racism at work and in their daily lives because they refused to retaliate to insults, taunting, and sometimes even physical abuses.

The situation is different with the Afro-Caribbean younger generation. The majority of them said they would ignore racism against them personally, only if such racism is not coupled with violence. But racism coupled with violence against them, their families and friends would be met with positive action, they will fight to defend their own. The younger generation claimed their parents allowed racists to get away with too much injustice against them. But they will not allow themselves to be trodden on physically. Some of the youths admit that there are terrible prices to pay for their resistance, such as imprisonment, and consequential stigmatisation. There is also the risk of possible injuries as a result of fighting. But they claim active resistance is inevitable because they are given no choice by the racists. Their lives and that of their relations and friends would be at stake if they refused to act. The youth of the Afro-Caribbeans justify their resistance by saying that non-resistant action could mean many more deaths and injuries to themselves and their people than when they put up brave resistance. Many of them believe that their resistance actually deters racists from attacking them more often.

One young man explained that he knows and understands that the physical resistance of racism is not the end of the black youths' problems. He is aware of racists whom they cannot fight physically. Those who discriminate against blacks at schools and in jobs. Those who hurt black people in subtle ways. He is aware that those people have to be dealt with possibly in the way their parents dealt with them, often to enable blacks to survive in their jobs. But he pointed out that such passive behaviour would only earn their generation contempt from their own children and grandchildren. They would not have made any progress in righting the wrongs with racism. They are aware that they are paying a heavy price for their resistance. But the price would be worth the efforts of the present generation of blacks if it contributes to the betterment of future black generations in any way. He said that if their parents had not been so passive about racism against them, things might not have been so grim for black people. He added however, that their parents cannot be completely at fault. They did their best in the circumstances.

The explanation given by the Afro-Caribbean day-centre clients about the gap between black and white clients and their Day Centres are well articulated and illustrated with convincing personal experience. But it may be argued that although racism and discrimination contribute to the poor provision of services to the black people's Day Centres, that answer by itself it too simplistic. There are other contributory factors. From the findings of this study, there is clear evidence that all is not well in the white dominated Day Centres either: there are complaints about organisation, premises, toilets, and quality of services. Examination of most of these complaints show that all boils down to poor and erratic financing. And yet the majority of these Day Centres play important roles such as keeping the young unemployed occupied to prevent their frustrations spilling into the streets.

So it is not completely fair to say that racism and discrimination is the only reason why the gap between black and white Day Centres exist. The white Day Centres have no problems about racism, and yet they also suffer from hardships. With the Social Services and the Local Authorities being cut back even further, it is clear that both black and white established Day Centres may continue to face financial difficulties, which affects all aspects of the running of these centres, unless a constructive remedy is found.

However, the crux of the matter is not how much the current government, or any other government cuts or increases funding for these Day Centres. The essential point is that regardless of whether the size of the national cake shrinks or increases in size, black people, like all other citizens, expect to get their fair share.

Women in Social Services Management

MAGGIE RILEY AND JULIA PHILLIPSON

One concern which practitioner-researchers have is that fieldwork divides important things up into insignificant little pieces. These bite-sized chunks are easily consumed but what, does the whole diet of findings add up to?

Practitioner-researchers, loosely speaking, are doing 'surveys' all the time. Through their daily work they collect impressions, check ideas and sense the deeper meaning of details. Yet bringing all the 'sense data' together is hard for two reasons. First, telling how it is' often rocks the boat. Secondly there is a struggle over the best way to do it.

Maggie Riley and Julia Phillipson are 'trainers' for women in Social Services management. They survey the scene with each course. Here they have chosen 'dramatic reconstruction' as the means of linking detail with in-depth discussion. They draw upon their knowledge and feelings to describe the intricacies which are involved in a seemingly innocuous request from a male Director. Dramatic reconstructions are particularly apt in institutional world which place great emphasis on roles. Reconstructions are pictures rather than proofs, pictures which can avoid thousands of words being spent explaining the obvious. They involve the reader directly and unavoidably in the tensions which are painful and yet have the seeds of radical change - Editors.

On Telling It How It Is

Just as women managers frequently feel that what they say about 'how it is' is neither heard, nor understood, nor treated as 'real data' so too with feminist knowledge. As Carole Ramazanoglu writes 'people are generally unwilling to believe what feminists say, not because feminism is 'bad' social theory, but because feminists' notions of what is 'really' going on in society, challenge dominant versions of reality'. They are politically and personally uncomfortable. 'We, as women who are researching and working with women, know that we are faced, within this text as well as in our everyday lives with the problem of how we make what we 'know' understandable and convincing to others'.

Understanding may come through acquiring facts, it may come from critiquing previously held assumptions, it may come from linking unique pieces of information into a wider framework, it may come from experience, it may come from empathic awareness. The routes to understanding are many. Some lend themselves more readily to the printed page and to the academic traditions particularly fact-ing, critiquing and theorising.

In what follows we offer you an alternative way of understanding what it is that we know. This is via an imagined scenario in which a group of women meet together to decide how to 'help' their male Director understand what it is like to manage as a woman, a request he has made of them. This we hope, will lead to understanding through the imagination and empathic awareness.[1]

One Afternoon in October

The conversation begins

Ida: *The Director wants to know `where he's got it wrong', he wants us to tell him what to do about the `problem' of women managers...*

Phyllis: *Perhaps it is really the problem of men managers?!*

Ida: *Yes, I know that, but since he has asked us, even if it is not really the question we would have wanted, it is a start - we have somehow to grab this opportunity and find ways of saying things to him in a way which will be heard, understood, and even better, acted upon.*

Heather: *Oh, that sounds oh so familiar, yet another exercise in translation; in having to make our voices heard in a way that doesn't cause too much stress on the listener. I'm so tired of having to do that.*

Jo: *And what will be done with whatever we tell him? Will it be used to confirm all those stereotypes about 'moaning minnies' and how women `can't stand the heat?' Should we expose our distress and the damage when much of the time we cope brilliantly?*

Ida: *It is not only a question of what we tell him, it is also a question of format. You know he wants a report to go to the monthly Departmental Management Group meeting, and no report for those meetings is ever supposed to be more than two sides of A4 long.*

Kate: *So we have to be brief sisters! Can we be reduced to two sides of A4 without doing ourselves a terrible injury...yet another case of women being shrunk to fit the ideal size and shape for man's consumption...*

Phyllis: *Perhaps we could do a presentation. WOW, now that would be something!*

Commentator: The Dilemmas

Imagine if you will, a group of women managers, of varying ages, and seniority in the same Social Services Department, meeting and talking together one winter afternoon. They have taken to meeting every couple of months to share news, survival strategies, jokes and to renew and replenish their increasingly crucial friendships. The county is a large one, only two of them work near each other, the others are scattered up to 70 miles apart. One or two of the women work mainly with other women - in domiciliary care and in residential care for older people; but for the others their being women makes them exceptional - two work in senior administrative and policy development posts at HQ and are the only women at that level, one has recently been promoted and is now, like three others, the only woman in her area management team. These meetings, with the opportunities for 'telling it how it is' have become something of a life line to them all, a chance to share the weariness and the humour, the outrage and the optimism so intertwined in their managing as women managers.

Now has come a summons from the Director, he has 'spotted' that the department has a problem - an imbalance of men and women at senior levels. He wants to be told why. From the why should follow the action plan: or so he seems to assume. It would appear to be exactly the opening the women have wanted and yet their response is neither immediate nor straightforward; a number of dilemmas cloud the path.

The Dilemmas Revealed
Why is he asking?
There could be a number of possible reasons, and there is a sense in which what we will want to hear will be determined by his reason for asking. If he is fundamentally concerned only with difficulties in recruitment and retention he may only want to hear about proposals for job share and workplace nurseries. If, however, he wants to grasp the nettle of sexism the changes would have to be about relations between people, about the culture of the organisation and so much more...So do the women try to cover all possible answers as to what might be amiss; do they emphasise what is important to them; or do they go for what they think he will hear?

Is it what we want to say or is it what he wants to hear?
How much should they learn about what it is like?
The norm of coping with the impossible is very strong in social work, indeed the ability to do just that is frequently taken as an indicator of competence and fitness for promotion. So to reveal that they experience difficulties in managing would lay them

open to being judged inadequate and not up to the job (and isn't that what many men think anyway?). And then there is the well established tradition of blame the victim. If the women talk about how they are ignored and ridiculed in meetings, how they are subjected to, at best frequent references to their personal appearance and at worst sexual harassment, if they show how they are having to prove their competence over and over again will they be believed? Or will what they say be taken as further 'evidence' of their weakness, their pettiness, their inability to be good women. If they share the pain will it be treated with respect and gentleness or will it be dismissed (even as they so often are) as irrelevant and exaggerated. To say only a little runs the risk that the reality of their lived experience is hidden from the men who will then be able to continue ignorant; to say a lot runs the risk of further damage, stereotypes confirmed, the private face made public.

Is it another plus male-minus female? Whichever way you choose it'll be wrong, there ain't no way that women can get it right.
How much can they speak for all women?

As white women managers they knew that they had access to power and privileges that the majority of women workers did not. Some knew what it was like to be a residential worker or a secretary because they had been just that, but none knew what it was like to be Black and to be experiencing racism on a daily basis. Many knew what it was like trying to juggle children and work, or work and caring for an ageing mother, but none knew what it was like to be lesbian or to be only three years off retirement with only a minuscule pension to look forward to. The differences between women were as important to get across as the similarities. How were they to make sure that they didn't silence the voices of all those other women and speak as if they knew it all, or as if it were the same for all women - in the way that men for so long had assumed the right to be able to speak for all mankind (including women in brackets).

One chant and many unsung voices, or many voices, many chants?
What language should be used?

As a group of women they recognised that the language of senior management was often alien. The men appeared to share a similar humour that was different - more competitive and bantering; they also spoke more of facts and less of impressions; more of tasks and less of relationships; more of objectivity and less of feelings. And if speech itself was different so, too, was the use of spaces between words and the listening to what was being said. As women they experienced the men as interrupting more; as challenging what had just been said - or ignoring it completely; whilst the women built on earlier contributions. The women listened with their eyes as well as their ears and saw what was being said with gestures and with expressions, with shrugs and smiles and yawns.

So the dilemma was should they try to 'translate' their knowledge into a language that they guessed the men would understand and respect? Would facts such as numbers of women to be found in different parts of their organisation be sufficient? Would an international perspective give more substance? Should they include quotes from 'unchallengeable' sources such as legislation? The 'rational' mode might convince the brains but would it 'win any hearts'? Could they indeed stay neutral when they felt so passionately?

To speak is not necessarily to be heard
In what form should they make their voices heard?

The dilemma of language was further compounded by the dilemma as to presentation. First there was style - punchy or humorous, serious and committed? Then there was manner of presentation - should it be impeccably presented on overhead projector with clearly typed information in different colours or perhaps information could be given out in advance of the meeting so that the time could be given out in advance of the meeting so that the time could then be spent in dialogue? Then there were issues about tradition. In the management meeting usually one person spoke to the agenda item under consideration; should they follow the tradition or change it and share the presentation? They would thereby make their difference visible. And was it only senior staff who could appear at such a meeting - could women representing different positions in the organisations appear?

The medium is (perhaps) the message

Time and place

Should they ask (argue) for the first slot on the agenda and a particular allocation of time? Should they let urgent issues and matters arising be settled first so that heads were cleared of pre-occupations before their 'slot'?

And what of the meeting place? The Director's office around a table with everyone always taking the same chairs could mean them feeling intruders at worst or guests at best; was there some way that they could create their territory and atmosphere.

Say it with flowers?

So many of their dilemmas seem to be about power. Power from tradition, from the right to define the issues, power from territory and the assumed right to speak.

They were being given some power but how much? Was it generously given or was it to be their only chance? Did they have any allies in the senior management group and if so how could they identify them and work with them - after all numbers are a source of power! The risk of being labelled extreme ('loony left' was a much heard term of abuse) could shift the power balance away from them again as a group and as individuals (would this ruin their careers in the organisation?). There seemed so many ways in which they might 'blow it'. And if they did what about other women who would be depending upon them?

And why should they be doing all this work and worrying and taking risks - why weren't the men doing some of it? Were they doing men's work -*again*?

Power imbalances between different groups of people can mean that those with less structural power remain muted, their experience ignored and silenced. Poverty, learning difficulties, disease, race have all been sources of and reasons for silencing what is often uncomfortable for those with power to know about. Women's talk has been disregarded by labelling it emotional or gossip, tattle or wingeing. It has been interrupted, ignored, ridiculed, despised. No wonder, then, that the pathway to public speech should be so clouded with dilemmas and uncertainties.

In answer to the request to 'tell me where we are going wrong', the women have to decide what to say and how to say it. Or else be silent.

Kate: *Well I say, let's go for it, stop agonising over the possible pitfalls and repercussions and `seize the moment'. Do you remember, that's what Margaret told us to do just after her husband had died and she still came to our last meeting - seize the moment. And we have one now. Lets plan what we might do and then think about what we believe will be most effective and what we believe we have the courage for!*

Heather: *Why don't we try a version of, well we could start with facts...like statistics. He would be impressed if we could stick in some demographic trends material on changes in the labour force as he is really worried about recruitment and retaining staff.*

Ida: I've got some good information from that conference I went to on Women's Position in Europe from the Equal Opportunities Commission. We could do that as handouts and on an OHP!

Clarice: I wonder if we could give them some different kinds of information, either as an exercise or as an illustration. There was that exercise we did in a mixed group where the men had to discuss who they went to with emotional problems, or when stressed, and the women did the same. And do you remember how the men said they all went to women, whereas the women went to women or men, (but more often to other women). That really highlighted form how women have to do much more work than men, especially in organisations like this, but also how men are less versatile than women!

Ida: That's a bit tough.

Jo: Yes, but real all the same. Let's hang on to that for a bit. What about getting some other kinds of facts. We could each talk to women in our areas, including secretaries, care workers and domestics and see what the issues are for them. That way we can cover quite a wide range of aspects of working as a woman and it would show the complexities.

Clarice: And it wouldn't look like just us finding life difficult!

Phyllis: Well I know in my area, when we changed offices there weren't enough parking spaces for all of us, so the admin staff weren't allowed in the car park on the grounds that they are `non-essential users', but of course many of them are women with small children in nurseries or with child minders etc. And having to walk from the public car park adds on an extra 15 minutes to each end of their day. The implications for them just hadn't been thought through.

Ida: Yes, that's a really good example. So what was your suggestion? We had some facts, perhaps starting with national trends and then some local facts. What comes after that?

Heather: Well I think what we really need are some examples, what they call `critical incidents', to help them understand what the issues are facing us, then we would need to move on to look at possible action plans. But unless the understanding is there the strategies for remedy will be inappropriate and / or sabotaged.

Kate: Or else they will all be things that they will ask us, ever so nicely, to go away and do!

Jo: Let's think of some examples.

Clarice: I'm quite happy to think of some critical incidents, in fact I think they could really make an impact, but I don't want the Director and those other senior managers to think that our life is all bad news, and I also think that it is important that we emphasise what skill and resources and personal *qualities we bring to the department, after all Social Services Departments wouldn't be able to function without women! Could we do some work on the critical incidents first and then go on to the positives?*

Jo: *That's fine by me; now what about some examples?*

Kate: *Part of the difficulty I'm having is how to get across that many of the aspects of managing as women that trouble us are small everyday occurrences, but they are cumulative and tiring. Then there are the whoppers, the jaw droppers. And there are those things that actually we just laughed at. Single examples just don't paint the whole picture.*

Heather: *Oh, yes, I can remember when you told us about your manager...how you had noticed that he was trying the `management by walking about' technique, and how he came into your room each morning to ask you how you were...*

Kate: *And if I said I was fine he would stay and chat, but if I said I felt low or stressed he would shoot off as soon as he could.*

Clarice: *Well we know what that means, because we recognise it immediately, would we have to explain to them that that is a really good example of how many male managers like to recruit strong women, and indeed lean on them, but want to disappear into the woodwork as soon as the woman in question looks a bit frail!*

Ida: *Shall we just try to think of some examples without sorting them, or we could start with a brainstorm of issues and then think of examples that go with them.*

Commentator: Still Trying To Get Past Go

So they did a brainstorm of both their strengths and the difficulties of managing. They looked like this (see overleaf). They stopped when the pages were full, not because there weren't other aspects that they could include, but because the pages were beginning to look rather crowded:

Heather: *Maybe we should all put in for a pay rise!*

Ida: *Come on, lets grapple with the difficult bit, what examples are we going to choose?*

Phyllis: *Isn't it hard to say it all in public, what are we frightened of? That the examples won't be `good enough'?' That however much we say or write we will still be told that they still can't see what it is REALLY like?'...That somehow we have failed again...this time to make it clear enough?*

Kate: *I just need to get started. I can't take standing on the water's edge anymore. So here goes. One of the things that happens to me is that because I have long fair hair, I'm always getting treated as a `dolly bird' by the men. I realised that whenever I have to go to a meeting where I will need to argue*

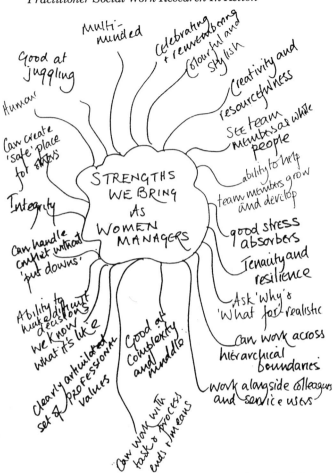

my point, I tie my hair back from my face. And for an interview I put on a severeish suit, and don't show too much leg. On the other hand, sometimes I think it is how much leg you show that determines whether or not you get the job! This doesn't sound like much, but what it makes me feel is that I cannot be myself, but have to be constantly managing what I look like. And the balance between looking 'too feminine' and therefore not a real manager, and between not looking feminine enough and therefore not a real woman, seems an impossible high wire act I'm always performing. And don't I wobble!

So femininity is always a issue in management, whereas masculinity is somehow taken for granted.

Being stroked or stroked touched

Being assessed like on what I look like or am Having to think about what I wear all the time

Not respected for my skills and knowledge, but

Expected to laugh at sexist jokes

Having to be strong, Criticised for it Always proving competence

Accused of being humourless

Assumed to be emotional

Interrupted or ignored in meetings

Emotions, mine and other women's treated as an irrelevant nuisance

DIFFICULTIES IN MANAGING AS A WOMAN

Having to survive accusations of being 'small minded'

Expected to mop up team members emotions & not trouble my male boss with them.

Not getting the supervision I need — I don't need to be TOLD what to do

Trivialised, ridiculed made to feel small and OUTRAGED

Most managers are men, do I have to be like them?

Expected to help him in my supervision

Not enough women around at my level to share issues with

Seeing the world differently

Speaking a different language

Clarice: I have an example a bit like that. Because I wouldn't join in the jokes at our monthly meeting, which were often about boobs or other parts of women's bodies, I was told I was a killjoy. Then one of the men said to the others, in my hearing though not to my face, that he thought my problem was that I wasn't getting laid enough. what was I supposed to say, or do for that matter. In fact I would really like some ideas...

Heather: Mine's a bit different from yours. I am really troubled at the moment by the meeting I have to chair. You know I took it over when I got my new job. There are about thirty people there, from health as well as Social Services and the vol orgs. There is one particular man who has made my life a misery. He kept ridiculing the way I chair and then looking round for praise from the others. He attacked me personally in the meeting, telling me I didn't know what I was talking

51

about, or that my ideas wouldn't work etc, he even told me I should go on a diet. I got to the stage where I felt I couldn't function. So I asked him to meet me for lunch one day. We met in a pub and he was really encouraging and pleasant and was full of how difficult my job must be, with having to get so many policies in place so fast. When it felt like the right moment, I explained that I found some of his behaviour in the meeting difficult. He agreed to stop, swearing of course that he hadn't meant anything personal. Well, I thought I had been really assertive, but also friendly. And do you know what he did in the next meeting - yawned ostentatiously; kept whispering loudly to the person beside him, or else just ignored me. I am getting to dread the meetings. And I'm usually good at chairing. I feel if it goes on I shall either get so angry and let rip or I will collapse in tears, either way I will end up looking ridiculous and not up to the job.

Phyllis: *Isn't it hard not to get caught up with each of these examples. I really feel for you both; it makes sticking to our task of just producing examples very hard. That may be a clue about any presentation. That examples like this generate so much emotion in us, and may produce a lot of either defensiveness or guilt in the men that they may not want to hear too much. I've got a less personal example, but one which I think shows clearly how many of the systems, which in theory have been set up to support women's equality are still being used to favour men. Shall I tell you about this one? Its not mine. I heard it from a woman who works in area personnel. She realised one day that a case of sexual harassment was being heard in her area later that same day. She also realised that all the people on the panel, of whom there were four and one of whom was her area officer were men. When she challenged him on this, he at first said he didn't see what she was making a fuss about, and then he said she'd got it wrong there would be a woman there. When pressed on this, the woman in question turned out to be the secretary, there to take the notes, not to take part in the discussion or decision-making. She got loads of the usual excuses about there weren't any other women available to sit on the panel, as panel members have to be at a certain level of seniority! So there wasn't much more she could do at that stage. Then to make matters worse, she found out the following day form one of the four women who brought the case, that although between them they had lots of examples of this man persistently harassing them all, the panel would only hear of one example; the most recent one. So not only were the women denied an audience of people who had some real understanding of what it is like to be sexually harassed over an extended period of time, by a man in a more senior* position, but most of what they had experienced was silenced. That way of course, the man can keep his good name, perhaps even enhance it, for being `one of the lads', or `liking his oats' is often seen as praiseworthy amongst men. The women, who presumably had been through all sorts of personal distress and took a chance with their careers to bring this case, must feel that the policies are, in reality, a mockery. And what do you bet, he will stay on and some, if not all, of those women, will feel they can't stick it here any longer. Oops, I'm beginning to get very angry. In fact outraged would be a more accurate word. And organisations like this call themselves caring and committed to social justice!

Jo: There are just so many examples aren't there. And we haven't talked about the way some other women, who have made it into senior management, can sometimes feel as damaging as men. Still, that is a whole other dimension. And to have to unravel what might have happened to such women that makes them behave like that is so complex...Perhaps we can build some kind of framework and then ask them to provide some of the examples that they themselves have noticed, perhaps they need to imagine what it is like to manage as a woman, rather than us having to spell it all out. After all, one of the things about sexism, and racism for that matter, is that it changes its face, its language and its behaviour. So the examples we give now might need to be different in a year or two. Kate 'On the other hand, an awful lot seems to stay the same. Especially double standards!

Commentator: Seizing the Moment - Speaking in Public

Making public, even in a safe group, examples of the daily bruising, was a painful business. For in order to survive in organisations they had learnt to pretend it hadn't happened, or to treat it as a joke - not serious, or is none of that worked, to hide away the incident even from their own recall. This way they rendered the incidents invisible or inaudible even to themselves. But the costs of such erasing were high for they erased part of what it was to be themselves. So there was a relief in sharing. Yet each woman felt the other's pain, a cumulative anguish.

Together they realised that:

To speak only on paper would not be a dialogue.
To speak as a solo voice was to lose the impact of many voices.
To stay seated around a table would not enable them to share the rich complexity of their understandings.
So they went for a presentation
Four women, of different ages and from different parts of the organisation although all managers, negotiate for a one hour 'slot'

in the management meeting.

They prepare overhead projector slides with well researched information.

The prepare some 'imaginative exercises' to help the group think their way into the issues.

They come prepared with some of the action that they think needs to happen, but they keep this in reserve, to compare with ideas they ask the group to prepare.

They share the leadership.

They recognise and use each others' talents.

They mix fact with passion.

They use the personal examples to identify the general issues.

They ask the group to think, feel, imagine and reflect before planning action.

They facilitate shared ownership of action planning.

They encourage even as they challenge.

They take risks in the hope that their risk taking may improve the world for others.

They do it all with style and humour and sensitivity.

But why should anyone be surprised by any of these things. They are just what women managers are doing all the time. And if they can manage all of this in a one-off session in a senior management meeting with its alien and ambivalent atmosphere into which they venture as invited strangers then surely the potential is almost unimaginable of what their speaking being heard may bring.

Footnote

1. This way is one of two ways. The second was by interweaving our and others theorising in and through the scenario. In this way we hoped not only to show, to explain and to convince; but we also hoped to integrate the symbolic with the factual, the subjective with the objective, the passionate with the prosaic and thereby provide a glimmering of the way in which feminist knowledge can be explored and validated.

Part Three
Investigative Studies

'The Children's Bedrooms Must Have Looked Very Pleasant When They Were Built': Perceptions of a Children's Observation and Assessment Centre

SIMON VILLETTE

This piece gives testament to the powers of observation and open ended questions as research tools. Simon Villette uses these instruments to unearth and reconstruct the realities of everyday life in a children's observation and assessment centre. He develops an understanding of this everyday life. The centre has a considerable impact on its youthful clients which either no longer recognised by its staff and planners as their 'reality', or is one which they avoid and have long ceased to question.

*'Unearthing', 'understanding' and 'reconstructing' are separate activities involving listening, locating key words and phrases and taking a responsible perspective on the diverse accounts. The attitudes of a method are equal in significance to its activities. Investigative studies depend upon whose 'reality' is being explained. Villette decided that the reality for the children is what should distinguish his account - **Editors.***

Context and Setting

The Children and Young Persons Act 1969 was a major reform of the social welfare provisions made by local authorities for children, particularly juvenile offenders. One of the most important changes it intended was to reorientate the traditional view of (I couldn't find this in the dictionary) juvenile offending behaviour, as criminality, towards a perspective which saw it primarily as behaviour which had social and emotional roots, thus requiring social work interventions. With this changed emphasis came the requirement under the Act for local authorities to provide facilities for 'observation' and 'assessment'. Section 36 (4) of that Act states that every regional plan should contain proposals:

...for the provision of facilities for the observation of the physical and mental conditions of the children in the care of the relevant authorities and for the assessment of the most suitable accommodation and treatment for these children.

In the early 1970s decisions were being taken by the then County Borough and County Councils concerning the opening of the observation and assessment facilities outlined in the Act. In the end a single centre was built. Although it received the Royal Assent in 1969, The Children and Young Person's Act did not become implemented over-night and it was not until almost the mid-seventies that it was in full effect in Northamptonshire. Prior to the implementation, Borough and County authorities had the old used remand homes, classifying schools in other counties, and reception homes. The latter were principally intended to take younger children requiring residence on welfare grounds but increasingly they were taking these older youngsters who were seen by the workers in such homes as 'management problems'.

One such home was established in an old Victorian detached house. It provided emergency reception facilities for up to 18 boys and girls aged 14 to 16 years. According to a former residential worker who went to work there in 1974: 'Its organisation was more like a children's home. The children went out in the evening. It was quite free and easy'. That particular social worker was to be one of the first to start at O & A Centre when it opened three years later. As time progressed the old reception home was taking more and more difficult youngsters including those who once might have been expected to go to the remand homes and classifying schools, as one staff member commented:

We were taking big beefy lads, really serious offenders. They were absconding and not turning up for court. The magistrates were getting fed up with us. Most of them were suspended from school, we had to try and keep them occupied during the day. Then we heard about the O & A Centre. We couldn't wait for it to open. We didn't really know what an observation and assessment centre was but we knew these lads were going to need more than we could offer to keep them under control.

The new centre, opened against a legislative background which saw it in terms of quasi-scientific diagnosis and an expectation by the people who would actually work in the centre that it would solve problems of management and control. Situated about six miles from the town centre the purpose built site was chosen so that the children, who it was expected, would come predominantly from the town would not be too far from their home communities. It was set on a north facing slope, overlooking open fields farmed by the neighbouring college of agriculture.

The tension between the Local Authority and the villagers epitomises the conflicts which arise from differing perspectives. On the one hand the Local Authority, contained within its context of statutory responsibility and a professional determination to do things properly, presents the attitude of careful and responsible decision-makers. They wish to be seen as sensitive to local feeling but capable of taking a broader view. On the other hand the local perspective was one of alarm that their equilibrium was going to be disturbed. Both groups were confirmed in their views by their respective cultures. On one side were the professional social workers and Local Authority managers. On the other there were the middle-class owner occupiers.

The intention of the Local Authority to create a home rather than an institution dictated the design developed by the architect. Using guidelines contained in an publication which lay down building standards for community homes (DHSS, 1971) a building was produced which blends in with the landscape and gives the impression from the outside of compactness. It was designed around a central spine running from the kitchen at one end to the classroom at the other. According to the architect it was intended that this should provide an area, central to the whole building, in which children could be worked with individually or in groups. He said: 'This area would be a constant source of activity and would give vitality to the building.' Branching off this spine were the two residential areas each of which provided sleeping accommodation for twelve youngsters and a sitting room. The children's bedrooms were on two floors and comprised a mixture of single and double rooms.

Although the centre was located in the most beautiful countryside the only windows which took advantage of the position were those in the north facing sleeping quarters which were unoccupied during most daylight hours, and the administration offices. The rest of the windows had no open views at all. As an architectural context it was shut off from the outside world, especially for the children. Equally, as time passed and the trees in the grounds grew, it was screened from public gaze from the outside.

A Loving Home or a Caring Institution?

As one entered the front door there was an entrance lobby with a staircase to the right leading up to the offices. To the left there was a door leading to the rest of the building. This distinction between 'upstairs' and 'downstairs' was felt strongly throughout the organisation. Comments like 'Them upstairs don't know what it's like down here' and 'The responsibility for managing the children is part of the task of the downstairs staff'. were often made; an example of how the architectural context can influence the language in which social relationships are expressed and cultures developed. Despite the intentions of the architect and the Social Services Department it was hard to escape the feeling that much of the building had developed as an 'institution' rather than as a 'home'. The hurly burly of such an environment meant that many items such as book cases and bedroom cupboards which were made of veneered chipboard were broken and proved virtually impossible to repair. Despite continuous efforts by social workers and cleaners, sitting rooms had an air of neglect with torn books and damaged records filling otherwise unused drawers and cupboards. There were few pictures and none which had been chosen by the children. There was a reluctance to have anything fragile on open display. Consequently there was nothing in the building about which the children could exercise any care. The wooden framed easy chairs were uncomfortable and lounging with one's feet on the plastic veneered coffee table was discouraged. It was difficult for the children to physically relax.

The children's bedrooms must have looked very pleasant when they were built. Each one had a fitted wardrobe, fitted drawers and a wash basin. Some had one and others had two beds. But soon many of the doors would be broken off their hinges and despite conscientious attempts to make repairs they did not fit very well and gave an air of impending collapse. The wear and tear of occupancy by the angry, the violent, and the frightened began to tell. One bedroom was so badly soiled by an enuretic boy for weeks on end that the carpet was removed and the room used 'for similar cases in the future'.

The children's beds had mattresses with an impervious cover to reduce problems caused by bed wetting. The result was a bed in which the children sweated because the surface on which they were sleeping did not allow air to their bodies. The floors throughout the building were thermo-plastic. The areas which were carpeted were fitted with a type of hard nylon floor covering often used in children's homes and homes for the elderly because spillages can be wiped up without leaving any stains. It is not the sort of carpet one would associate with the comfort of a family house. It was as if the centre had been built to be indestructible, like an adventure play-ground or a padded cell.

Just as the fabric of the building suggested an institution rather than a home, the language of the organisation bore greater similarity to that of the prison or the hospital than it showed distinction from it.

For example the sleeping areas were referred to as 'wings', the sitting rooms as 'day rooms' and the largest component of the communal area was known as the 'rec room'. The children were sometimes confined to their wings for bad behaviour. This was known as being 'winged'. Such language was shared by both adults and children. Far from using the central communal area as a 'constant source of activity' as envisaged by the architects children were herded from the wing to the school room, to the dining area and back again as if they were prisoners being transferred from one block to another in a maximum security jail.

Just as it was difficult to avoid the sense of the building being an institution, it was difficult to ignore the way in which it operated to contain and control. The windows were supposedly designed to prevent children climbing out of them by being too narrow. When the children broke the catches so that the windows would open wider they were fitted with chains. When this did not deter attempts at climbing out some of the windows were nailed shut. When the children broke the windows in order to get out toughened glass was recommended.

From early evening the front door was locked. In the depths of the night this may seem a reasonable precaution against prowlers. However when an excited group returned from the swimming baths at 8 pm to be greeted by a locked door it did little to give any sense of welcome. Occasionally the sleeping quarters were locked during the day so that the children could not go to their bedrooms. This was one of the issues over which the children got the most angry. Whenever the door to the bedrooms was locked they responded with resentful comments about not being trusted.

Every time a member of staff wanted to go into the staffroom they had to unlock the door. As one worker in the centre commented:

Keys? They're everywhere! On several occasions I have been sitting in the staffroom and as someone has gone out they have locked it with me inside! One member of staff carries his key on a leather thong attached to his belt like a prison officer. I was never more aware of the significance of locking doors as one evening when I was alone in one of the sitting rooms shortly after the children had gone to bed. At ten o'clock the member of staff who stays awake during the night, known as the 'Night Waking Lady', arrived on duty. She let herself in through the front door and then an inner door, both of which were locked. She must then have found the kitchen and staffroom doors unlocked because I heard her lock them. In the silence the sound of those four locks being turned echoed through the building like some ghostly gaoler in Newgate.

Sounds seemed to be amplified in the building by the high ceiling in the central dining area. This is the principal thoroughfare from the entrance to the building to the living areas. The absence of soft furnishings, a hard tiled floor and the use of metal serving dishes made mealtimes sound like an iron foundry. The plates and cups were of plastic, some of them stained and marked with cigarette burns. Because the utensils were unbreakable the children tended to throw them around. This was seen by the adults as the justification for keeping the plastic tableware.

People and Perspectives

The building was the product of a number of people and their individual perspectives. The architect had his view of what a good community home was, based on the DHSS guidelines and his training as a designer. The professional administrators and social workers knew what sort of building they wanted to meet the tasks as they saw them. The local politicians knew that they had to provide these facilities to meet their obligations to the electorate and the law, and at the same time 'keep the villagers happy'.

The product of these perspectives was a building which contained and isolated the children from their home communities and the locality. As a context for the children it represented 'being locked up' or 'sent away'. To the adults it was where they 'did a shift' or 'came on duty'. For all of them it was where they tried to survive:

You know you are shut away and there's no going home. All you can do is try and get through it as best you can.

You clock on and do your shift, counting the minutes. You do anything to get by without feeling as lost and as helpless as the children.

Children's Views

As with the staff, the children, felt the institution's powerful impact on them. Some of them felt abandoned. They saw themselves as 'locked up' or 'shut away'.

I'm shut up in here 'cos I can't cope in my family. My social worker is going to get me out and into a foster family.

Being in here is like being in prison. There's rules for everything. When I get out I'm going to smoke all the fags I can get and eat what I want to and go out with my mates...All the things you can't do in here.

I've been here for ages. Never seen my social worker.

I don't know what is happening to me. My social worker makes all the decisions. She never listens to me. I'm just the one it's all happening to. I'll be the last one to know what's going on.

On the other hand many children enjoyed being at the centre. Regardless of their understanding of the reasons for being there, their actual experience was of a place which was good to them.

It was good there. I know we mucked about a lot but the place was alright. We had good laughs even with the teachers. Some of the staff were a bit 'moany' but you get that everywhere. It was certainly better than the boarding school I used to go to. No one would ever talk to you there. At least there you could find someone to talk your problems over with.

It was nice having people around you all the time. I liked it there. It was easier than being at home. You never had to make any decisions it was all done for you. We all used to complain about having no freedom there but we were glad really that the staff kept us in line. It's no good when kids do as they like all the time.

The staff there were great, at least some of them. You could con fags out of them and mess around rotten but they would just carry on. Once or twice they got real mad but the next time they came on duty it was like normal.

Reflections

The centre existed in a number of different forms and at a number of different levels. It had its public appearance of a quasi-scientific source of information. It had its private function and first priority, (its 'hidden curriculum'), of keeping the children under care and control.

At the level of individual experience it was a place in which to be 'shut away', to feel intolerable anxiety, or to be relieved of a problem. At the level of personal change it is hard to say precisely what impact the centre had although it was a place that always had some impact. For example as one ex-staff member stated:

I enjoyed working there. It was an important part of my life. We were doing some useful things for the kids, if only by showing them that we cared and would carry on caring even when it got tough.

In terms of impact on the children it is easy to pick on the instances where things go wrong such as the child who came to the centre because he was being beaten up by his father and who leaves twelve months later with a criminal record having been enticed into an episode of car stealing with another lad. It is easy to recall the case of a girl who was admitted because she was out of control and running wild with an ex-prisoner of whom nobody approved. She ended up totally dependent on the institution and incapable of living independently. She was then discharged into the community to do little more than 'fend for herself'.

On the other hand it was the same centre which received that girl back again after she was sexually abused in a hostel for vagrants and it was the same centre which provided a secure home base while children took O level and CSE exams. It was the centre which made one former resident comment:

I wouldn't be here now if it hadn't been for the place. I was running around with a really bad crowd. Most of them are inside now. I know I went to Detention centre, but going back there afterwards gave me a new start.

In the documents written before the centre opened no one considered that children might pass through the place more than once, that they would stay for months on end or that it would be the place to which children would be sent who had nowhere else to go.

Yet that is just the way such centres are used. The primary task of 'being assessed' was almost incidental or so it seemed to the child's experience in the centre as part of their teenage career.

Hidden Problem Drinkers in Probation

Eric Knapman

This study's starting point is an assessment of hidden problem drinkers on Probation Service caseloads. The word 'hidden' strongly suggests that the first all-important step for practitioners is to discover whether the problem exists. Such a discovery necessarily involves the acquisition of individual assessment skills - but it involves much more. Knapman shows the critical factors, personal and organisational, which combine to weaken the work done by autonomous professionals. It is also likely that the ambivalence shown by the Probation Service working with `drinkers' reflects a wider ambivalence about the management of alcohol usage in society.

The vital contribution of this piece is the detailed way in which the author begins to discover the differential assessment and treatment of problem drinkers and hidden problem drinkers.

*The text is more concerned with developments than with discovery. Nevertheless it is apparent that Knapman has invented a screening device which takes 10-15 minutes to use and yet could alter practice for months and years to come - **Editors.***

Let me begin with outlining the scale and nature of the problems of 'problem drinkers' according to data I collected, compared with other data.

Table 1
Male Probation Clients' Drinking Levels Compared with National Findings for the General Male Population

Age Consumption (units per week)	18-24	25-34	35-44	45-54	55-64	65+	All Males (over 18)
Probation Service Clients (N = 97)	31.3	50.3	22.7	21.7	1	-	32.2
General population*	28.1	22.4	20.3	20.3	15.7	11.7	20.3

* According to DHSS National Survey, n=713.
One unit of alcohol is the equivalent of 1 single pub measure of spirits, 1 small glass of sherry or fortified wine, 1 small glass of table wine, a quarter pint of strong beer, lager or cider, or a half pint of ordinary beer, lager or cider.

Male probation clients exceed the national average in all age groups except the two oldest. The most significant group is the 25-34 year olds where instead of following the trend to decrease in each age group these probation clients show a considerable increase and drink over twice the national norm. This group averaged 50 units or 25 pints per week. Both of these figures represent a considerable amount of cash spent on alcohol. The majority of the clients were unemployed (68%) at the time of interview suggesting potential financial problems if nothing else. The volume of drinking suggests that for some cases drinking had reached a level at which physical harm was being done. The level of consumption of alcohol is said to be a key indicator of whether individuals are in danger of developing long term health problems which arise from excessive drinking. Consumption of alcohol above 50 units a week was considered excessive in both this research and the DHSS Survey.[1]

This survey done by me used the same criterion as the DHSS Survey when seeking to identify other alcohol problems. These were problems of a physical or psychological nature. Physical dependence meant clients were drinking first thing in the morning, they had shaky hands the morning after and there had been occasions when they had been unable to stop drinking. I also used the physical criteria of being either drunk or sick through drink more than three times in a three months' period to define a physical problem if coupled with self report on any of the three physical symptoms given above. The psychological problems posed were questions on whether the clients were annoyed by criticism of their drinking and whether they felt they ought to cut down on their drinking. If the clients acknowledged having two or more of these physical or psychological problems then they were identified as problem drinkers both in this research and the DHSS Survey. I also took the officers' statements that the client had committed offences which were in some way drink related as an indication of a drink problem.

In my survey, out of the 182 male probation clients interview, 102 or 56 per cent were identified as having a drink problem of some kind. In examining Table 2 the scale of this problem is highlighted with the term 'no drink problem' cases' and `drink problem cases' is used to describe clients as they were identified initially by the probation officers. In Table 2 some 65 cases, or 47 per cent of clients, in that group are shown to have a drink problem where previously officers had not identified them as such.

Of the 182 males interviewed 102 revealed that they had some kind of drink problem. The figures are quite staggering. It is not so much that probation officers disliked these problem drinkers, it is not that there was insufficient support and reward for working with them nor was it in their lack of confidence. It was their inability to recognise the problem amongst their own clients, that is the critical issue. If they had identified it then they had certainly not portrayed it as a problem to be worked upon.

Table 2
The Identification of Drink Problems of Male Probation Clients Interviewed (N = 182)

	Male Interviews	Drink Problems Identified in Survey Interview	Recognised by Officers as Having a Drink Problem
	(n=182)	(n=102)	(%)
No drink problem cases	139	(65)	47
Drink problem	43	37	86

If the figures for men and women which I gained are combined it suggests a level of non-recognition over those 205 cases interviewed of nearly 45 per cent.[2] I am not talking of alcoholics or those physically dependent upon alcohol, but people whose lives in some part are affected by alcohol to the extent that problems arise. These can be manifest in physical or psychological areas or through offending.

Non-Recognition or Suppression\Avoidance of Problem Drinkers?

The discovery of such a high level of non-recognition raises some fundamental questions and revived my original supposition that suppression might be taking place.

The failure to recognise problem drinkers even at the developing stage may not only be a failure in diagnostic ability or suppression due to lack of treatment skills but possibly an expression of what Davies (1974, p.100) has described as that recurrent paradox of social work, namely its ability to serve best those who least need it. Thus if one does not have the ability to deal with the problem, it is possible that one avoids identifying it thus avoiding any advertisement of failure.

Non Recognition: Differential Interventions or Perceptions

I had set out to discover whether there was anything particular about these 'drink problem clients' or the officers' work with them which might throw some light on their failure to be recognised. What I discovered, though an examination of 63 cases of unidentified or hidden problem drinkers was that staff disliked working with them slightly more and had a lower level of contact with them than the general caseload. Also unlike the identified problem drinkers, they were more likely to be in the low rather than high category of offenders. Could it be, due to the methods used by probation staff? I examined these 63 'hidden problem drinkers' in the same way as I did for the 'problem drinkers' and found that there were some differences in the distribution of methods being used. Table 3 below sets out the details.

Table 3
Methods Used by Probation Officers with Problem and Hidden Problem Drinkers: A Comparison

Methods of Probation Intervention	Identified Problem Drinkers	Hidden Problem Drinkers	Total Caseload
	n=193	n=63	n=1434
Advice and direct guidance	46%	43%	41%
Support	33%	24%	32%
Reflective discussion	26%	22%	22%
Ventilation of feelings	29%	13%	24%
Authority or control	19%	17%	15%
Monitoring and surveillance	11%	21%	17%

From these figures it would appear that these 'hidden problem drinkers' cases are treated in a slightly different way from either the identified 'problem drinkers' or the general caseload. The 'hidden problem drinkers' were given less support, allowed to ventilate their feelings less often and are more likely to be supervised by a technique described as monitoring and surveillance. What each of these methods entail may vary between officers but they were accepted within the research by the respondents without any need for clarification. Support tends to be expressed in a variety of ways but generally stems from a warm and empathetic attitude by the worker. Ventilation of feelings is a self-evident technique which implies a degree of willingness on the client's part to 'open up'. The monitoring and surveillance role is almost a euphemism for watching what the client does but not having a great deal of influence over him. How these clients came to be missed by officers might then have been due, at least in part, to an unconscious suppression of the evidence that they had committed drink related offences, a failure to engage the client in direct discussion about his leisure interests and a style of supervision which tended towards an observational role rather than an interactive one.

Hidden problem drinkers are twice as likely to be seen less frequently than other clients as Table 4 shows.

Table 4
Contact Levels Between Probation Officers and Problem and Hidden Problem Drinkers (n=1434)

Selected Client Categories	Level of Contact		
	Low	Medium	High
Problem drinkers	30.6%	32.1%	37.3%
Hidden problem drinkers	63.5%	28.6%	7.9%
Total caseload	30.2%	40.0%	29.8%

The clients whose drink problems were identified through the interview sample are far less likely to be in frequent contact with their probation officer than other clients. There may be factors in these cases which influence judgements apart from drink problems. Clients may be able to hide their drink problems from officers through a low level of contact. This could lead to less officer satisfaction and a failure to establish the kind of rapport which is necessary to ask the more searching questions about their social behaviour and alcohol use and abuse.

Finally, I looked at the criminal history of these 'hidden problem drinkers'.

Table 5
Criminality Levels of Hidden Problem Drinkers, Problem Drinkers, and Total Caseload Calculated from Previous Convictions

Selected Client Categories	Number of Previous Convictions		
	Nil	1-4	5+
Hidden problem drinkers (n=63)	20.6%	71.4%	8.0%
Problem drinkers (n=187)	10.7%	31.6%	57.7%
Total caseload (n=1277)	20.2%	44.4%	35.4%

The total caseload is mainly in the lower criminality level whereas the majority of clients identified by officers as problem drinkers are in the higher category. In contrast those who have been discovered as having hidden drink problems are overwhelmingly in a lower criminality group. This suggests that one of the factors which alerts officers to the question of a drink problem, as an aide memoire, could be recurring offences.

Failure to Identify Problem Drinkers as an Organisational Issue

The major organisation difficulty for the Probation Service is that organisational goals, however well intentioned and legitimate, can be modified and developed into quite different goals by the probation officers who implement them. Figure I attempts to show some of the major decision areas influences policy and practice areas.

Figure I
Organisational and Personal Influences on Problem Drinking Practice and Policy Issues in Probation Work

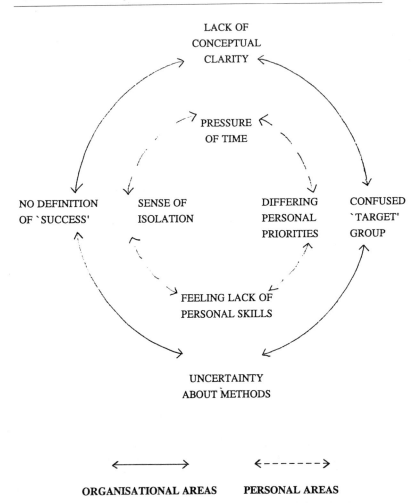

The inner circle represents the areas most likely to be felt by an individual and the outer represents those more likely to be organisational areas. They are interchangeable and the order of flow does not necessarily imply any sequence of occurrence.

Areas which are organisational must be contributed to by individuals. They are put forward in this way to demonstrate how they interact with one another. For example, whilst the organisation might lack conceptual clarity, the same could also be said of individuals.

The failure of the Service to define a 'target' group or define 'success' in whatever terms, leaves officers with a sense of isolation which they combat by defining their own priorities.

Likewise, the choice of methods is one which the organisation could help to clarify through providing training courses and from publishing research into the relative effectiveness of differing methods.

The Way Forward

Having established the extent of hidden problem drinkers on the probation caseloads it remains to examine the reasons, within and beyond the individual probation officer's control why there is such inaction in this area, and what can be done to improve this situation.

At the time of my research there had been a number of research studies and government policy initiatives concerning drink problems in this country, and the voluntary sector's and the Probation Services actual and anticipated role.[3]

Some of these recommendations for further training, more research in alcohol assessments, and greater work load allowances for probation officers dated back to an earlier report (in 1971) and probably before then as well. There are also issues about the status of alcoholism and problem drinking and drink driving as social problems as well as the Probation Services' proper place in wider social policy debates. My research also confirms Crolley's (1981) views that probation officers tend to diagnose the drinking problem 'too late' (i.e. when drinking patterns are very apparent and firmly established).[4]

Yet its 'under-diagnosis' by probation officers, and the clear scale of hidden problem drinkers on probation caseloads also suggests this is a sufficient problem to be higher or the services list of priorities. Then, to add to a highly complex and confusing overall picture there are the conflicting views held by practitioners that social workers and probation officer's already have the necessary skills (Bennett, 1982, p.31), or that they do *not* have them (Todd, 1981, pp.7-8) to identify the problem. In other words, there are a range of factors internal to and outside the Probation Service which affect its capacity to assess drinking problems and problem drinkers and treat and help them. Ultimately, it can be argued, work with problem drinkers depends on individual staff commitment. If this is the case *should* it be the case? It can also be argued that the organisational framework within which officers work remains an equally critical determinant factor. However, whilst the 1970s was a time of service growth and service diversity (whether or not this included providing a priority service to problem drinkers), the current climate is of 'tougher', more centralised and accountable objectives consistent with those of the overall criminal justice system. In such a climate it is difficult to see problem drinking, as a category in its own right, getting the priority it deserves.

Working with the Problem: Ideas and Practical Tips

Within the Probation Service there is a core of committed and enthusiastic individuals who are prepared to work with this issue. It is from their enthusiasm and upon their commitment that the development of this area of work depends. It is a realistic expectation that every officer should be able to diagnose, if not treat, this group of clients.

The 'Early Recognition' Ideal: Training and Support

The initial step is to develop a level of awareness towards the latent problem drinker through early recognition. It is the probation officers that have to take the first steps and some relatively easy form of recognition needs to be available and used. The concept of turning clients away from further offending through active intervention is a well accepted task of probation officers. They are only too well aware of the patterns of behaviour which point towards the dangers of reoffending, for example, peer group influences, breakdown in relationships and financial pressures. There are similar signals which point towards a deterioration in drinking behaviour and which should stimulate activity on the part of officers to assist their clients.

There have been questionnaires which identify individuals as having alcoholism with almost perfect accuracy (see for example, Stockcrell et al., 1979). It has not become standard practice for probation officers to use check-list methods but, I consider that this research has pointed to the value of such an approach. A checklist method of scanning cases for latent drink problems would take only ten to fifteen minutes. This could identify the extent of alcohol intake, by probation clients at an early stage of their contact with the service, explore its physical psychological/ emotional, financial effects, and lead to individual casework plans being made.

The development of an early recognition notion for problem drinkers should not be allowed to stagnate at probation officer level. There is a need for the whole organisation to ensure that all cases are scanned at team level and some follow-up devised which leads to improved diagnosis and specific treatment programmes. The management response should be focused on establishing and sustaining the scanning processes, providing training and offering support.

It has been demonstrated that failure to recognise problem drinkers on existing caseloads is an area of major concern. If the first step towards improving the involvement of the Probation Service is to recognise them, then the second step is inevitably to improve officers' confidence in working with them. It seems less helpful to simply call for more training opportunities without providing a support system for staff engaged in this work. There seems relatively little one can do about this apart from encouraging staff to persist with this work, if possible, alongside more experienced colleagues.

A support system would be most effective if there was a specialist within each probation team. In Northamptonshire Probation Service at the time of my research, work with problem drinkers developed rapidly in teams with 'specialists'. One of the findings of this research was of ambivalent feelings about management support, especially in relation to an attitude that management could do more. The provision of training courses would go some way towards meeting that expressed need.

The call for research in this area has been made almost as often as the call for training. There are small pieces of research which probation officers have conducted which have had only limited distribution. The growth in information officers within the Probation Service indicates a developing awareness of the need for processing knowledge. It is a development which should continue and be recognised as a valuable use of resources. The monitoring of effectiveness in terms of probation officers work with this group of clients is a function more likely to be carried out thoroughly if management is committed. The National Probation Research and Information Exchange or any regional groups with a similar purpose should also be used to collate these research findings which could be linked into other research which is taking place in other agencies.

In relation to drink problems there is a need for teams, areas and the Probation Service as a whole to identify more clearly the size of its alcohol problem and the response it is making to it. This can be carried out through local surveys. They would be more useful if gathered using some generally agreed procedures rather than in the present piecemeal way.

The Probation Service needs to become more involved in the national debates which are taking place in relation to alcohol abuse and its contribution to the national debate will be that much more substantial if it is backed up by researched information. In order to do this effectively, a national information gathering exercise needs to be undertaken and a more standardised and deeper level of enquiry is needed.

Concluding Comments

My research has identified some of the major obstacles to the development of a fully professional response by the Probation Service to the problem drinker. It has demonstrated the high proportions of clients likely to be involved and supported the idea of greater support at team level by the appointment of a specialist worker. It has also endorsed other recommendations for more standardised research, and training.

My call is for an early recognition notion to be adopted by the service in relation to problem drinkers and for staff to be sensitised to the issue. The anticipated improvements in local practice are likely to lead to demands for greater knowledge and the exchange of information should be developed at local, regional and national levels leading to a national working party on the issue. In a nutshell probation work with clients with alcohol problems needs a higher priority than it has hitherto been given and needs to be informed, based on the sorts of research evidence I and others have unearthed, for practitioners, and policymakers alike, and lead to full policy implementation and national debate.

Footnotes
1. The Royal College of Psychiatrists in their Report (1979), *Alcohol and Alcoholism,* suggest specific levels of consumption above which there are risks of damage and likely dependence. Whilst they accept that different people react differently, they do offer the provisional level of 56 units for men. (pp.52, 140, 141).
2. The figures contained in Table 2 relate to males. The number of women in the survey was very small and those findings are not included here, but, in any case, are almost identical to the men's findings in the table.
3. Royal College of Psychiatrists Report (1979); Christian Economic and Social Research Foundation, Agenda for Action on Alcohol (1981); Kessell Committee Report on Educational Training (1979); DHSS *Homelessness and Strategy for Research on Alcoholism* (1980); DHSS National Voluntary Organisations and Alcohol Misuse (1982); Working Party Report on Habitual Drunken Offenders (1971).
4. *Editors' Note*: Without screening as Knapman has done, it is probably very difficult to identify problem drinking at an earlier stage when clients fail to disclose it as a problem, become defensive if challenged, and when the offence is not drink related.

Reflecting on Research Methods Piloted to Investigate Activity Groups in Probation

BOB BROAD

This piece describes the ways in which research methods were developed and adapted to investigate activity groups. The key question was how could the experiences, interactions, attitudes and actions characteristic of groups of people engaged in practical tasks be monitored and recorded? The entire research period was spent developing ways of answering these complex questions and\or revising the question! Had time allowed, further studies would have built on and adapted the methods outlined here. There was a real sense of urgency to complete the work on time and research schedules had to be maintained, promises made to the potential research customers about visits, methods and objectives had to be kept, and deadlines approached.

*There are two main points. First a multiplicity of research methods is desirable, to fully record and cross check the accuracy and validity of emerging data. Second, the importance of the practitioner-researcher being flexible, and experiencing and learning about research methods during the pilot stages of a research study. The research methods reveal hitherto largely unknown interactions that characterise activity groups, and the data produced raises policy questions about the status and management of activity groups in probation work - **Editors.***

Introduction

Activity groups in probation usually take the form of motor projects, adventure weekends, bicycle workshops, Day Centres and supported work schemes. Whilst seemingly starkly different from conventional individual casework approaches they are also similar in that they offer scope, support and potential for clients to gain insights about and change their behaviour. My research had a commitment to focusing on the experience, operational stance, and policy implications of activity groups within probation work and sought to learn about the problems and potential involved in this approach to probation work. In particular I wanted to pay attention to these groups' credibility and accountability issues in terms of providing a supplementary way of working with offenders, mostly young offenders. I also set out to analyse the function and value of activity groups, and begin to even tread that thorny path of group evaluation, going beyond client attendance figures. This piece outlines the methodological routes I developed and highlights some provisional fieldwork findings.[1]

Developing Methods

The exploration into the substantive content of activity groups began with an examination of a government funded workshop for young offenders. I then developed pilot studies in three further activity groups settings. Here I want to concentrate on the methods developed at and applied to two of those activity groups, a workshop for young offenders, and a probation run motor project for young motoring offenders. In turn I will take the reader through the various methods I employed in the pilot studies. These pilot studies eventually produced replicatable research instruments for examining activity groups. These research methods are listed in Diagram A below.

Diagram A
A Typology of Activity Group Experiences and Methods

	Behaviour	Attitudes	Skills
Individual	1	2	3
Peers	4	5	6
Supervisor	7	8	9
Research methods	Sociograms changes check-list	Open-ended questions, questionnaire	Participant observation

This model provided the eventual framework within which three principle elements of activity groups were analysed; interpersonal behaviour, formal and informal content, and peer/staff attitudes. In this piece I will concentrate on describing sociograms and the changes checklist, because these were developed by me specifically for this piece of practitioner research. Although the model incorporates both a behavioural and attitudinal approach to examining activity groups, its main emphasis is on observable behavioural aspects of activity groups. The emphasis given to this 'behavioural approach' was deliberate and was considered to be most suitable for groupwork which focused almost exclusively on activities. Sociograms provided a way to examine propositions about the behavioural characteristics of activity groups and served to bring the minute group processes to visibility.[2]

I hoped to answer the questions: 'What do group members get from attending this group?' and 'What does belonging to this activity group offer beyond performing the activity itself and completing the required tasks?'. Two propositions pointed towards sociograms as one suitable method. The first was that behavioural interactions give an indication of group member's feelings about themselves as individuals, their peer group and those in authority, namely supervisors. The second was that in such groups there is likely to be a degree of change (personal growth and/or regression) over time which can be observed and recorded by monitoring the nature, style and frequency of interaction.

Sociograms provided a means of assembling snapshot records of behaviour. The principle advantage is that they enabled one to see patterns of interaction at a glance. A distinct advantage is that they could be continually up-dated, thereby providing a picture diary of interaction over time. Diagram B is a basic sociogram illustrating interaction between three people in a group A, B and C at one point in time.

Diagram B
An Example of a Sociogram Recording Interaction in a Small Group

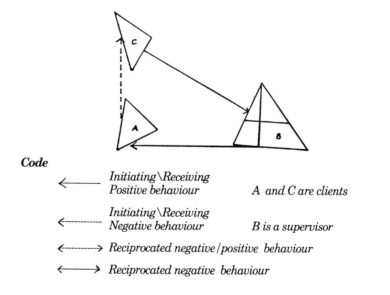

Code

⟵——— *Initiating\Receiving*
 Positive behaviour   *A and C are clients*

⟵------- *Initiating\Receiving*
 Negative behaviour   *B is a supervisor*

⟵--------⟶ *Reciprocated negative/positive behaviour*

⟵————⟶ *Reciprocated negative behaviour*

Positive behaviour included:- laughs, shows satisfaction, agrees, showing acceptance, gives and understands instructions, complies with requests, shows friendship, gives support, touches in a positive manner (e.g. hugging), gives suggestions and directions, asks for suggestions and directions, suggests possible ways of action, is helpful, is cheerful.

Negative behaviour included:- disagrees; showing passive/ active rejection of methods/help; withdraws when approached; is hostile; is verbally aggressive; is threatening; touches in a negative way (e.g. hitting or slapping); shows antagonism; deflates other's status; displays unhelpful behaviour such as playing up or fooling around; shows indifference; is sullen when asked something or is approached.

During a one week period at the first pilot project, an assembly workshop for young offenders, I observed the interaction between group members by means of a series of sociograms similar to the example given in Diagram B. Sociograms were drawn at 30 minute intervals and at the end of the week transferred on to one recording sheet providing a summative sociogram for the week. At the end of my period at this first pilot I had 50 sessional sociograms. My first problem with the sociograms was deciding how to present and analyse them. Firstly I transferred all of them onto one sheet producing a summative sociogram for the week, and secondly I reproduced the data from the summative sociogram in a matrix form (see Tables 1 and 2). This form allowed me to more systematically plot the direction and scale of responses between group members. These matrices present negative and positive behaviour, the categories having been derived from the original behavioural types used for the sociogram and built up on the summative sociogram. The two matrices clearly indicate who is initiating what sort of behaviour to whom and identifies the recipients of the different types of behaviour.[3]

Table 1 then is the matrix of positive behaviour.

Blank squares represent no one initiating/receiving positive behaviour (i.e. in effect nil positive interaction).

Although all the group members are recorded on Table1 the scale of interaction is exceptionally sparse. The tasks (picture frame\jewellery assembly work) required minimal interaction and the group responded accordingly. Incidents of friendly interaction were fleeting, almost unnoticeable. It was significant that only five out of the 23 employees indicated positive behaviour from one other, and in seven of these nine cases no other interaction was recorded between them. I now want to present and examine the negative behaviour matrix.

Table 1
Positive Behaviour Matrix Indicating the Direction and Scale of Group Interactions Observed at a Workshop for Young Offenders During a One Week Period

RECEIVING BEHAVIOUR

INITIATING BEHAVIOUR

	a	b	c	h	m	n	o	p	q	r	s1	s2	u	x	e	pt	d	gr	
a		2									1			3			1		a
b	2																1		b
c														1					c
h		1																	h
m																			m
n						3													n
o							2												o
p						2	2												p
q																			q
r										1									r
s1								1			1	1							s1
s2																			s2
u	1		1												2		2		u
x																			x
e																1			e
pt																	1		pt
d																			d
gr	1																		gr
	a	b	c	h	m	n	o	p	q	r	s1	s2	u	x	e	pt	d	gr	

INITIATING

RECEIVING

1 represents initiating / receiving positive behaviour once.
2 represents initiating / receiving positive behaviour twice, etc.
u, s1, s2 and pt are work supervisors, the remainder are employees.

Blank squares represent no-one initiating/receiving negative behaviour (i.e. in effect nil negative interactions).

This matrix also enabled me to decipher and analyse patterns of interaction. With the exceptions of group members X and A, and staff member Pt, group members only instigated negative behaviour on one occasion towards another member. Group member 'A', who occasioned the most negative behaviour was regarded as 'a problem', and 'disruptive', and was told to leave the project the week after this part of the research came to an end. It transpired that he was suffering from some form of psychiatric illness and regularly returned to hospital for treatment. Although the four staff members (U, S1, S2, and Pt) initiated negative behaviour to group members on only three occasions, they received negative behaviour from group members on seven occasions. The negative behaviour expressed was often in response to the tedium of the tasks rather than the snarl of the

Table 2
**Negative Behaviour Matrix Indicating the Direction and
Scale of Group Interactions Observed at a Workshop for
Young Offenders during a One Week Period**

RECEIVING BEHAVIOUR

	a	e	'2	h	n	s2	pt	d	u	s1	x	
a			8			1				1		a
e						1						e
'2												'2
h										1		h
n									1	1		n
s2												s2
pt		2										pt
d												d
u								1				u
s1												s1
x	1			1					4			x
	a	e	'2	h	n	s2	pt	d	u	s1	x	

(Left axis: INITIATING BEHAVIOUR; Right axis: INITIATING)

RECEIVING

1 represents initiating/receiving negative behaviour once
2 represents initiating/receiving negative behaviour twice, etc.
u, s1, s2, and pt are work supervisors, the remainder are employees.

supervisors. What also emerges is the relative isolation of group members from one another. When not working on the formal tasks, members interacted more freely. In trying to establish overall patterns which emerged from the data, it was noticeable that those who initiated and received negative behaviour mixed with others who did the same. A further interesting observation from the data is that the only people who were the recipients of negative behaviour and did not initiate it were the supervisors themselves. What emerges from the data is that the sociograms identify and the matrices record those people initiating and receiving positive or negative behaviour and also identify groups, small cliques, social isolates, and popular group members.[4]

Whilst I was at the workshop recording the sociograms I was seen by some of the clients as somebody of whom to be suspicious and comments towards me included 'We're not fucking specimens, you know', and 'Oh yes, you're the informer'. The supervisors generally regarded me as a confidante and the management group (sited on the ground floor of the two storey building) saw me as a potential ally and source of information, for example, 'What is really going on upstairs?'. Although the 'results' of this first pilot study were not startling they did allow me to understand ways in which others could use sociograms to record small group interaction, as a way of informing small groups about their behaviour, and consequences for group members and institutions alike. Despite then collecting these sociograms about group interaction and experiences, it became clear by the end of this first pilot project that in order to explore and record group experiences more rigorously further methods needed to be devised, as illustrated earlier in diagram A.

Evolving Approaches to Measurement

In examining these matrices within the context of this first pilot project, at a jewellery and picture frame assembly workshop it became apparent that the individuating nature of the tasks had the effect of separating and not uniting group members. Although the more withdrawn group members occasionally received extra help from staff, intervention was in the form of an instruction. The emphasis upon individual and not group learning excluded any potential for personal growth within a group context. Responsibility was firmly located outside the group and individuals were responsible for their own and not others' behaviour. Sanctions (official warnings, pay docking) and rewards (work and attendance bonuses) were allotted on an individual basis, by contrast with the motor project, the second pilot project.

In addition to my participant observation of individuals and the workshop group, I became interested in two phenomena which I had not originally planned to include in the study. First, the informal comments people made about the project seemed important and second the culture of the project particularly its rules and norms needed recording.

Therefore for the second project, a motor project for young offenders, whilst continuing with the sociograms, I decided to extend the time spent talking with staff and client groups in a more structured way (see Diagram A) in order to ascertain their views and feelings about the project. A series of open-ended questions provided the basis for examining staff and group members' attitudes. These questions were designed to discover to what extent statements about project objectives concurred with observed operational practices. Guttman Scalograms, devised as a way of drawing out the groupings of attitudes, built on answers to semi-structured questions and proved a most useful additional research instrument.

A further investigative method (built on sociograms) was a checklist of anticipated and actual behaviour and involved staff making assessments at the client referral stage, and subsequently, to record actual client developments. Essentially this 'changes checklist' itemised various questions about behaviour and asked the social work staff member referring the client to the activity project, (here a motor project) to rate the client's anticipated development areas whilst at the project. The project supervisor was also asked to do the same assessment both after an initial client interview (prior to joining the project) and once the client had been at the project for a set period of time.[5] Table 3 presents the changes checklist form sent out to staff.

Table 3
An Example of a Changes Checklist Designed to Record Anticipated and Actual Changes in Behaviour at a Motor Project

A. In their relationships with other clients do you think the client will

Item No.	Possible Development Areas	Very Strong	Strong	Irrelevant	Weak	Very Weak
1	Be easily led					
2	Make friends readily					
3	Show frequent hostility					
4	Be inclined to bully					
5	Be withdrawn					
6	Take the lead					
B. In himself do you think the client will/did						
1	Increase self-worth					
2	Attend regularly					
3	Extend their attitude to life					
4	Learn practical skills					
5	Go through any other changes. If any which you think are likely					

Note
This same form was used both for anticipated and actual changes, therefore the wording of the items needed to be amended accordingly.

This changes checklist was used in one motor project and recorded changes over a one month period, although a longer period was initially seen as desirable, time permitting. Not surprisingly perceived client changes during attendance over such a short period of time were minimal. What was significant was that of 63 responses given about actual behaviour 55 showed 'improvements' or 'no change' over the one month period with just 9 indicating 'deterioration'. These provisional findings seemed encouraging, suggesting that even in a short space of time motor project in question, positively affected clients behaviour whilst present, despite the inevitable proliferation of influences, good or bad, external to the project. In other words it suggests that whatever else the motor project achieved in practical terms it did more good than harm in terms of personal and social development. Equally exciting was my discovery of the hidden paths to certain behaviours, (in diagram C) referred to as a critical path analysis of activity group behaviour.

A Critical Path Analysis

A critical path analysis illustrates the various desirable and undesirable 'flight paths' individuals may take. Here these behaviours were directly derived from the preceding changes check list and built on ideas developed with the sociograms. The data suggests that social 'spin-offs' for individuals in activity groups only occur first if they attend regularly and second if they acquire some sort of practical skills beyond the basic ones.

Route A (see overleaf), the regular attendance route, was encouraged and fostered as staff sought task fulfilment and group maintenance functions, and valued the goal of group members having an opportunity to become peer group leaders, and possibly team leaders.

The changes checklist and critical path analysis were then important so far as the management of activity groups and their outcomes are concerned in terms of identifying critical paths to be encouraged and discouraged.

Summary

This piece then has, illustrated the ways in which various research instruments were piloted to record the experiences and management of activity groups in probation. The other two activity groups recorded in the study (Broad, 1982) were Probation Day Centre work and weekend adventure activity groups.

It is worth recording here that at the Probation Day Centre

Diagram C
A Critical Path Analysis of Activity Group Behaviour

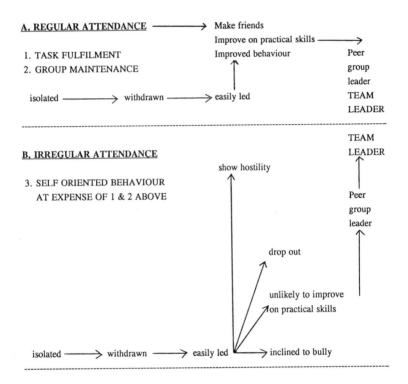

as well as at the workshop, the staff group were fascinated to see the recorded staff and client interactions as produced by my sociograms and keen to identify the personnel involved to understand the 'real' state of relationships there'.[6] This response, plus others from my feedback to staff about their views, attitudes, working assumptions (as recorded through semi-structured interviews) and observed actions were especially important and exciting aspects of this piece of research.

Finally a word about practice, management and policy issues. It is no coincidence that the more positive interactions and changes took place in a motor project which members were not obliged to attend. The more negative and minimal interactions took place in one case in a more coercive probation setting, in another a low paid workplace (see earlier Tables 1 and 2) where repetition and routine 'outvalued' personal creativity and growth. In other words this sort of practitioner research not only answers certain sets of practice questions, it also provides clues to broader management and policy questions - here about the value, nature and purpose of activity groupwork in a variety of social work settings.

Footnotes

1. Broad (1982) *Activity Groups in Probation* MSc Thesis, Cranfield Institute of Technology.
2. Moreno used sociograms principally as a way of recording inter-personal choices in groups.
3. Bales used a more systematic and detailed approach when collecting his data and he further categorised the various responses into sets of either social-emotional, or task-based areas.
4. The recording of these interactions subsequently led me to consider broader issues of power in social work groups building on social control, social justice and social welfare models of group work. The paper which built on these ideas entitled *The Uses and Abuses of Professional Power in Social Work Groups* (Broad, 1991a) was produced for the First European Symposium on Groupwork, Imperial College, London University, 18-19 July.
5. Clients were not aware that behaviour monitoring was taking place because such an awareness could have acted as a change agent in itself. However if taken beyond the experimental stage, in ongoing practitioner research, I would now recommend that the changes checklist findings could and should be shared with clients. Early in the research partnership, too, clients could be involved in drawing up the criteria for and monitoring of such changes. But this involvement could well affect any subsequent account of that project's impact on clients whilst in attendance.
6. The remaining method employed to explore the various phenomena in activity groups was participant observation to ascertain the group's content and the practical life skills on offer.

Dealing With 'Mad' Clients

RICHARD MITCHELL

*Investigative studies may take the form of finding out what 'the services' feel like to clients and what their career paths through `treatment' and tasks can be. Richard Mitchell picks up the pieces of a different jigsaw. Here is an account of an emergency team, Barnet, when faced with `madness'. The guiding literature is interwoven with emergent questions. The quest is to discover the pattern of responses to behaviours which are `mad'. What customs and practices have emerged over time? What do tables of data tell us about these embedded practice habits and 'mores'? Mitchell returns and returns to seemingly chaotic data. He reveals the categories and coping strategies of the team's social workers for whom mad behaviour is a normal experience - **Editors.***

Mechanic (1962) claims that basic decisions about the original diagnosis of mental illness are made by lay people, not doctors, the psychiatric profession's task is to confirm this. The value and accuracy of psychiatric diagnosis of madness have always been steeped in controversy (Bentall, 1988). One could well argue therefore, that the lay definition of madness is an important if not the most important part of the process of becoming a psychiatric patient.

Even if I had wanted to, using the medical definitions of the various sub-categories of psychotic illness would have presented me with considerable problems. The most important of these is the fact that clear medical categorising of people referred to the Barnet service seldom happens. Only six of the total sample that I interviewed had acquired a medical diagnosis for their condition. This surprising fact may simply expose shortcomings in administration but alternatively could demonstrate how the methodology and philosophy of the service has affected medical practice.

My working definition of madness is therefore 'behaviour that a reasonable person would consider to be mad'.

As I interviewed each social worker and client I indicated those clients that clearly could be considered as having been mad using the above definition. I included only those clients where the mad behaviour was the prime reason for them being referred, as opposed to those with only a previous history of madness, and where the social worker had tried to work with that madness. Some examples of the behaviour I am referring to are as follows:

> She was acting really bizarrely, gesticulating, making funny noises, really weird. She wore a strange ballgown-type dress and kept hitting her boyfriend on head...He didn't seem to mind (sw).

> I became manic, I was hallucinating. I got into the Festival Hall where the Police Federation were meeting. I wanted to tell them I was Jesus' (client) - He was the maddest person I had ever come across up till then (sw).

> I heard Paul Daniels on the TV say I am going to take your son. He told me to take off my wedding ring and put it outside. I was supposed to sit outside as well, which I did. That's when the police were called (client).

I identified eight by this method.

The Eight 'Mad' Clients

A therapeutic interaction between social workers and people suffering from acute forms of madness is a rare occurrence. A closer examination of what happened will obviously be of interest and hopefully of value. Table 1 lists all the 19 clients who were interviewed, arranged in ascending order according to the frequency of social work visiting (column I).

Column II gives my assessment of those who were exhibiting mad behaviour[1] Column III is a judgement made by each social worker about whether or not they considered their client to be in crisis at the time of referral. Column IV tells us whether or not the client was a first time referral to any psychiatric service or had a previous history. Column V shows if the client was admitted subsequent to referral. Finally Column VI shows the social worker.

Five of the eight social workers are shown as working with the eight 'mad' clients (Col VI), the same five define some of their clients as in crisis (Col III). The fact that my sample produced these particular social workers could be a purely random event of no significance. However, four of these five social workers show a distinct preference for brief interventions. Further it is the same four social workers who feature in an excluded 'one offs' group and who clearly must be using criteria that allow them to evaluate their work in terms of a single encounter. So immediately we have a sketch of some of the qualities used by the social workers in working with clients who experience madness.

Table 1
Clients Arranged in Social Work Duration of Contact Order

CLIENT	I	II	III	IV	V	VI
A	1-4		CRISIS	IST		SW 1
B	1-4	MAD		PRE	ADMIT	SW 5
C	1-4	MAD	CRISIS	PRE	ADMIT	SW 5
D	1-4	MAD		PRE		SW 5
E	5-12	MAD	CRISIS	PRE		SW 6
F	5-12	MAD	CRISIS	1ST		SW 1
G	5-12			1ST		SW 3
H	5-12	MAD	CRISIS	1ST		SW 4
I	5-12			1ST		SW 1
J	13-36			1ST	ADMIT	SW 4
K	13-36	MAD	CRISIS	1ST		SW 2
L	13-36			1ST		SW 4
M	13-36			PRE	ADMIT	SW 6
N	13-36			1ST		SW 4
O	13-36			1ST		SW 6
Q	13-36			PRE		SW 5
R	36+			1ST		SW 7
S	36+	MAD	CRISIS	PRE		SW 5
T	36+			PRE		SW 8

Key
I   *Duration of contact*
II   *Clients exhibiting mad behaviour*
III *Clients considered by their social worker to be in crisis*
IV   *Clients who are first time referrals (1st) or with previous psychiatric*
     history (pre)
V   *Clients who were admitted*
VI   *The social worker*

In Table 1 Column III, we see that seven clients from the total sample were considered by their social worker to be in crisis at the time of referral. Six of those in crisis are also defined by me as mad. This would seem to imply a relationship between the two. Social work involvement with the mad group tends to be briefer (Col I). With six of the eight, social work involvement had ceased by twelve weeks. This would tend to reinforce the notion that the social workers were working with this group as if they were in a psychosocial crisis.

Individually what can be drawn from the above points is limited, but together they begin to suggest the method used by the social workers in working with clients exhibiting madness. The social workers included a preponderance of those who preferred to work short term and who tended to evaluate what they did in terms of a single event. They also tended to equate mad behaviour in terms of a life crisis.

The most striking data in Table I lies in Column V. Only two of the eight were admitted to hospital where psychotic behaviour of the type that I have described above would commonly result in admission.

So let us look at the issues raised above in more detail by looking at the interviews with the eight 'mad' clients and their relevant social workers.

Madness, Crisis and Furore

The relationship between my definition of madness and the social worker's definition of crisis came as quite a surprise to me. I had expected to find the opposite; that crisis work would be carried out mainly with the sad neurotic client.

Despite the common use of the term there appears to be no consensus as to what actually constitutes crisis intervention (Hobes, 1984), or indeed even what a crisis might be (O'Hagan, 1986, p.14). The theory of crisis intervention based on the work of Caplan lies at the heart of the Barnet model, but to a large extent they have developed their own methods of working. Although there are similarities with other crisis intervention services, in this area, too, the Barnet system seems unique.

The team is structured to respond quickly to crisis. The social worker gains access to clients, in this case exhibiting madness, in their home at a comparatively early stage of the development of their problem. Crisis intervention is, of course, also central to the thinking of the social workers, defining a case as a crisis has a particular significance to them. So how does the system work in practice?

First let us look at the 'mad' who were not in crisis since this might help us understand more about those who were. In six out of the eight clients where madness was present the social workers also considered there to be a crisis, this of course means that two cases fell within a 'non-crisis mad' category.

What Was the Difference?

The two non-crisis clients who experienced madness were, in fact, both clients of the same social worker. They both had long previous psychiatric histories and the social worker used the expression 'furore' as opposed to 'crisis' when discussing them. The term furore was first described by Farewell (1976), one of the consultants involved in setting up the Barnet service. A furore effectively presents exactly as a crisis, but differs in that what is occurring is not new. Rather than being a fresh incident it is a repetition of a previously unresolved crisis, some times of a previous generation, but this time before a new audience. Farewell thought that these furores could occur many times, eventually becoming a way of life unless there was a concerted intervention plan.

In fact the way that the two furore cases were handled did not differ from the techniques used in crisis. The only noticeable difference lay in the social worker's lower expectations and aspirations for the client:

It was more of a furore. A chronic patient acting up again in a way to get herself admitted. This meant that I was less committed to work it as crisis case. I was not as concerned about the outcome. It just didn't seem worth putting lots of effort into a well known patient acting out again (sw).

This client, who was one of the two who were admitted, had a very different view of what happened:

My mum was always in and out of psychiatric hospital. That had an affect on me. I was really afraid I was going like her...They asked me lots of questions. I just wanted to get away. I didn't think they would put me in hospital again. I should have gone to a woman's refuge (client).

It is unfair to judge this concept of Furore on such a small sample of one social worker's work. It would appear, however, that the term can become another 'labelling' word which in turn may help create the very 'stereotype response' that it purports to describe. The implication of the above is that something new or different needs to be happening for the case to be considered a crisis.

In the six remaining examples of madness, which we shall now examine in more detail, examples of recent life changes were evident. The social workers clearly saw this as a key factor in relating crisis to madness. There appears to be an established relationship between life events and psychotic behaviour that leads to admission to hospital (Brown and Birley, 1968). It must not be surprising that the social workers were attracted by this concept. They may, of course, be open to the accusation of over simplifying what they found, by assuming that life events must therefore cause madness. It demonstrates, however, that social workers were looking for therapeutic ways of engaging with a group of people who are often thought to be not worth such effort (Litz, 1987). Let us look at the effect.

Normalising Behaviour

With the six mad/crisis cases there was quite a distinct pattern in the way that the five social workers reacted. Their prime goal seemed to be to 'normalise' the strange behaviour. This entailed giving explanation to that behaviour within a psychosocial framework and attempting to imply meaning within the context of the clients' own life:

> *I saw it as a man failing to face major life issues about separating from parents and who was handling the stress by going mad. I felt it was really important that he did not see himself as a mental patient and therefore not able to deal with these issues. I normalised what was happening as life issues. It was important not to focus on symptoms (sw).*

At times this appeared to be an effective technique. For example, with the lady who had been told by Paul Daniels on the television to sit outside, the social worker was able to help the couple connect the content of the television programme with the tragic loss of their son in a cot death several years earlier:

> *I now realise that this was part of the problem. It was just dreadful to hear it said (on the television programme) that parents were responsible for cot death. I felt how do I go out of the door, people would say I got rid of my little boy. I used to think of him but we never talked about it.*
>
> *After he died I used to get very scared about my two other sons. Every little bump, moan or groan and I would examine them from head to toe. I used to drive them crazy doing it over and over again. Sometimes I would keep them home for weeks. I was so afraid something would happen to them...(becoming very distressed). I still find this so upsetting. I can't talk more (client).*

However there was also evidence that social workers felt it so important to make this connection that it was tantamount to a personal failure when they could not do so. For example, following the one crisis call that resulted in admission:

> *This left me feeling really dissatisfied. I just offered admission. I tried but I could not get to what was going on underneath (sw).*

Again we are touching on the criteria by which social workers judge themselves.

Reducing Anxiety

The second major group of techniques used by the social workers working with clients who experienced madness could be grouped under the heading of 'anxiety reduction'. Whether or not madness is associated with a high degree of anxiety in its sufferers, it most certainly generates anxiety within the immediate family and social network. The social workers saw the reduction of this to be vital to the success of holding the situation at home.

I saw the immediate issue as containing the effects of his behaviour, of making people feel safe. I had to manage this by making sure that they knew that someone would be there if needed. I especially tried to reassure his wife. She was prepared to help if she felt supported. I considered that she was the key, if she collapsed, he would collapse. My aim in all this was to decrease anxiety.

The main thrust of the social workers' early intervention is therefore widened from the individual to the family or network. Indeed as much effort might be put into supporting the relatives as the person experiencing madness.

The social workers appeared to be giving a high priority to providing a sense of containment. The most common method of achieving this was by frequency of visiting. In five of the eight 'mad' clients initial contact involved visiting more frequently than weekly (Table 2). In two cases, clients F and K, this entailed daily contact. With client H and K very frequent visiting continued for four weeks. With the rest the frequency had reduced to weekly after ten days.

Another method of reducing anxiety by containment was to give 'direct access'. Direct access meant that any family member of specific named members were allowed to call the duty crisis team at any time of the day or night. It is interesting that when this was given it was much appreciated, appeared to have the desired results helping to lower tension, but was used by only one of the sample.

Table 2
The Pattern and Frequency of Social Work Visiting to the Eight Clients Exhibiting Madness

CLIENT	LENGTH OF CONTACT	FREQUENCY OF VISITING	SOCIAL WORKER
B	1 OFF	1 OFF	SW 5
D	2 WEEKS	WEEKLY	SW 5
C	3 WEEKS	WEEKLY	SW 5
H	5 WEEKS	< WEEKLY	SW 4
E	5 WEEKS	WEEKLY	SW 6
F	12 WEEKS	< WEEKLY REDUCING TO WEEKLY	SW 1
K	16 WEEKS	< WEEKLY REDUCING TO WEEKLY	SW 2
S	104 WEEKS	< WEEKLY REDUCING TO > MONTHLY	SW 5

Although it is my intention to focus on social workers, there was one important aspect of containment that necessitates other disciplines and needs to be referred to here. The early anxiety reducing phase often involved medication. Its use seemed to form an essential part of the technique. This, of course, required the role-exclusive skill of doctors to prescribe it and at times the monitoring skills of CPNs. For this reason alone, we can see the need for a multidisciplinary approach to coping with madness.

I do not have any examples of circumstances where the social worker attempted, yet failed to establish a crisis programme, but I must assume that this happened at times. The examples I do have, however, seem to indicate that, despite initial misgivings, the approach is very much appreciated by clients and their families.

At first I wanted admission. I thought that was the only answer and they were closing the door in my face. My view soon changed when I saw how much (sw) was prepared to do. I got the impression that I could see (sw) or someone from the team at any time I wanted. I never abused this, even although there were times when I wanted to. Knowing that someone would be there just made such a difference. When I think what could have happened....It would have been so bad for me if I had been admitted and even worse for my children. I have nothing but praise for the (sw)'...(client).

Of course not all clients were prepared to give such adulation but three made appreciative comments about this containment phase of the help they received and no one criticised it. Problems, when they occurred, came later.

Admission

It is important to bear in mind that the most common first step in the medical treatment of people who exhibit the type of behaviour that I have just described would be admission to hospital. (Kaplin et al., 1988, pp.253-303; Busfield, 1986, p.51). The admission rate to the unit as a whole is significantly lower than one would expect for our catchment area and population. It is possible that the containment that I have described is one of the core processes in preventing what would otherwise appear to be an inevitable admission. How far do the two cases who were actually admitted confirm or refute this idea?

With these two admissions there did not appear to have been any attempt by the social worker to set up such a containment programme. I can think of three reasons as to why this did not occur. It is possible that the behaviour was just so extreme that there was simply no way that it could be contained in the community. One of the two did show bizarre behaviour but no more so than others in my sample. The behaviour of the second admission was not so extreme.

Another explanation, as we have seen above when we looked at 'furore', is that the social worker could predetermine the outcome by holding the view that, in these particular occasions, it was not worth trying. Both those admitted did have previous psychiatric histories but only one was described as furore.

A third alternative comes out of the circumstances of the initial visit. There was something distinctly different about these two calls. In direct contrast with the six who were not admitted, both were not seen at home, one was interviewed in a police station, the other in a casualty department. The social worker could not have such easy access to the family and local networks. Options for providing containment were therefore substantially less than those who were seen at home and not admitted. The circumstances of the admissions could then be seen to support the idea that being able to reduce anxiety by giving a sense of containment is a significant factor in preventing admission.

There is, however, one more reason why this containment of anxiety is so important. Madness is medical territory and the social workers know this. Culturally, even although the Mental Health Act allows them contact, they are not expected to be 'working' with people in such a state. This view is even reinforced within their own profession. Madness is usually a semi-public event, the neighbours know, the police might be called in, the General Practitioner (GP) is there, many people are aware that something strange is happening and the pressure to 'do something' is intense. In such a volatile environment the social workers are aware that if they do not take the heat out of the situation and produce some results quickly, then their claim to be able to help will be seen as spurious. The social workers' anxiety is therefore also likely to be high. Containment not only helps to reduce this but is vital to the process of legitimatising the social workers' claim to work with madness.

This group of techniques in conjunction with the 'normalising' of mad behaviour described above comprised the initial methods used by the social workers in working with madness.

Follow-up Work

So what happened after this first phase of crisis containment? If we look back for a moment to Table 7 only three of the eight cases were closed by four weeks.

Just one of those three was also considered a crisis. In the remaining five mad/crisis cases social workers continued to be involved for from five to one hundred and four weeks. The containing and normalisation work that I have just described must therefore have been only part of the overall package being offered by the social worker.

I have used the term 'containment phase' in order to help define what appears to be an important area of social work practice. Describing what happened as a phase is, however, a little misleading because it gives the impression of one phase ending and another beginning. In fact I could not distinguish a time when this happened. While the social worker was attempting to work with mad behaviour then containment seemed to be a part of what was offered.

Although, as described, in the initial contact efforts were made to normalise the mad behaviour, in the early stages at least the social worker would often not probe any further than this. Working with such issues in any depth was though likely to raise anxiety and therefore be incompatible with the aim of its reduction:

At first I did not attempt to look behind at what was happening, they just couldn't have taken that. It would have raised tension so much that the whole plan would disintegrate (sw).

Any working on the problem was left until anxiety had reduced enough to make admission less likely. So while admission was a possibility anxiety reduction was the main goal of social work intervention.

Normalisation as I have already stated describes an attempt by the social worker to reframe the mad behaviour in terms of recent events in the client's own life. The move to working on the problem seemed to be marked by a reduction in emphasis in containment and an increased concern with these life issues.

The degree to which this happened varied. In general and not unexpectedly, the longer the case was open to the social worker the greater the depth of this working on life issues. (A significant exception to this was client S, the one long term client in this group that was referred to above).

In client H for example containment was the bulk of the work that was done and visiting was frequent throughout the five weeks of contact:

I felt that if he could get over this crisis, there was enough social connection for them (the couple) to function. So I aimed to get him back into his system as quickly as possible and make it a short term case. My focus was mainly rebuilding his confidence in carrying out practical tasks and reducing tension. We did a little work with the family problems but not much (sw).

It is interesting that it was this 'little bit of work on the family problem' that was most remembered by the client as having helped:

It was our discussions about the family that stuck in my mind. It really helped and it was comforting that someone else could understand. I thought (sw) was getting to the root of my illness (client).

The most detailed and complex work was done with client F and K, but even here there were variations. The containment phase was over by two weeks with client F, where as with client K it still continued at four weeks, stopped then started again for a short period. It seemed that containment and working on the life event issues were inversely proportional.

Footnote
1. Using criteria developed elsewhere in this study Mitchell (1990).

Parenting Children With Physical Impairments: The Process of Realisation

Investigative studies are particularly suited to the interface between people with special needs and the professional responses to them. At this interface a process takes place, people work out what is happening to them and what help they should or could get. They almost become para-professionals in this respect. At the same time, though, professional actions and attitudes can be awkward, anxiety-adding and antagonistic. So there may be distance and defiance compounded with an acknowledging deference.

*Anthea Coghlan reconstructs the process of realisation which occurs in parents who have children with physical impairments. They 'find out', experience a disruption of expectations and change their perspectives on 'time'. By locating and looking at different factors Coghlan investigates the learning of those who 'already know' and those who 'gradually discover' - both processes in which professionals play a vital part - **Editors.***

The Process of Realisation

Parents gave very varied accounts of the ways in which they had come to learn of their children's impairments and the process by which they came to understand the nature of their disabilities. Here the term, 'realisation' indicates that part of the cognitive process through which parents come to recognise how their children are different from most other children and the implications of their differentness. It is a gradual process even though, for some parents, the initial discovery is sudden. Realisation involves the re-ordering of parents' personal constructs of parenting. It has a dynamic quality and evolves through time so that parents' established perceptions of their children are continuously subject to re-evaluation as they grow and develop.

This table shows the frequency distribution of the ages of the children at the parent's initial discovery of their physical problems.

Table 1
Frequency Distribution of Children's Ages at Parents' Initial Discovery of Their Impairments

Age of Child	Numbers of Children
Birth	23
0 to 6 months	7
7 to 12 months	5
1 year	2
2 years	0
3 years	2
4 years	1
5 years	2
6 years	1
7 years onwards	0

The average age of the children at the parents' initial discovery was ten months. Of diagnoses, 58 per cent were made before parents began to realise that their children had impairments. In the case of parents who discovered their children's impairments over a period of time, there was an average delay of one year and four months before professional acknowledgement of diagnosis. The average time from parents' earliest discovery or suspicion to the time of the interviews was five years.

In twenty one cases there were prenatal or perinatal problems which caused some concern about the well-being of the children around the time of birth and it can be assumed that, for these parents, the process of realisation had begun even before the birth of their children. Parents were sometimes warned by the doctors attending them that their children might developmental problems, but the nature and extent of their difficulties were not necessarily known to either professionals or parents at this time. The parent's realisation of the impairments was a gradual process over several weeks, months or years. Their descriptions of how they came to know that their children were impaired are illustrated below:

Table 2
Parents' Discovery of Their Children's Impairments

	No of Children
Diagnosis at birth or soon afterwards	18
Sudden illness causing impairment	7
Diagnosis made later in child's life	7
Gradual discovery of impairment before professional acknowledgement	11

The future implications of the children's impairments varied according to the type of condition and its effect on heir individual physical development. Parents described their current understanding of their children's prognoses as follows:

Table 3
The Children's Prognoses

Prognosis	No of Children
Improving condition	4
Uncertain future progress	22
No change expected	11
Deteriorating condition	6

For the majority of children, their future progress was uncertain when taking into account the possible impact of their increasing physical maturity, intellectual growth and emotional and social development. Even for parents who were told at their child's birth of the likelihood of impairment it was not always possible to give a clear diagnosis and prognosis and they often found that the true nature of the impairment, as it intruded on their children's everyday lives, was only gradually revealed to them. Louise's mother recalled her experiences after her birth:

She was born three months early and she had a brain haemorrhage. We knew within a few days that she'd be handicapped but they didn't know to what degree. They didn't think it would be really bad so it was a matter of waiting to see. She had hydrocephalus at about ten months old and they were very worried at the hospital but we were very lucky and it tended to right itself. She went for all sorts of tests and they said everything was ok. There was nothing to worry about, the damage had been done and there wasn't going to be any more. It was dreadful, I know there was this worry about hydrocephalus. Of course, for months I kept thinking her head was swelling. It was terrible. It wasn't until she was ten months old that they discovered that she'd got cerebral palsy, only because she wasn't doing things that normal children do. She wasn't trying to roll, crawl, kick or splash in the bath. We didn't know how handicapped she might be. Before she was two she hardly spoke. I was very worried because I thought it was a mental problem. But she's coming on all the while.

The Initial Challenge to Parents' Personal Constructs of Childhood and Parenting

Cunningham and Davis (1985) write that, when they have children, parents develop a construct model to make sense of the world. They anticipate the events of childbirth and childhood, their own behaviour in relation to their children and to their trajectories as individuals and collectively as families. Cunningham and Davis argue that the origins of the constructs are within parents' own childhoods and in their previous experiences and an unelaborated construct system quickly develops and evolves to make sense of their children and of their circumstances. On the other hand, parents of children with special needs face at least one major disruption to the construction of a clear anticipation of the child's development and behaviour and of the nature of their role as parents. Many of the parents who tool part in this research described this experience. Sarah has hydrocephalus and balance and coordination problems. Her father illustrates:

> *You have a vision of what it's like when you get married, all your friends have got it right. Two handicapped children and made redundant three times and it was fast going the way it shouldn't have been going.*

At diagnosis, or at parents' initial suspicion of their children's physical impairments, existing personal constructs are invalidated or challenged. Parents can only draw on whatever past experiences which they currently find meaningful. Cunningham and Davis argue that, where parents have little knowledge of other children with similar special needs there is initial uncertainty, confusion and vulnerability.

Berger and Luckmann (1966) write that if a person is faced with problems which have not yet been routinised the process of incorporation of knowledge and skills required for a new task begins as the individual seeks to integrate the problem into everyday life. Sarah's father went on to say:

> *We'd never had contact with handicapped children. The wife always thought she couldn't cope. I couldn't handle handicapped children but I can now. I used to feel pity and get flustered. I could never watch anything on television about handicapped children. I couldn't handle it but I can now. It's a good experience to have. It's totally different when you have one.*

It was deduced from the data that a small number of parents used previous experiences of parenting, of physical impairment and other knowledge to develop their new constructs but that most had no basis for the establishment of their understanding of their children and their impairments other than their continuing direct experience of their care, which evolved through time. Even useful previous knowledge did not soften the blow of discovering a physical problem, or diminish the resulting challenge to or invalidation of parents' existing constructs and the need for reordering of expectations and for the re-establishment of new methods of parenting.

The Nature of Parents' Discovery of Their Children's Impairments

Thirty two sets of parents learned of their children's impairments, at birth or later, from professionals. The remaining ten sets of parents experienced a gradual realisation that their children had physical problems. There were reported differences in the ways in which these two sets of parents reacted to their experiences.

The Sudden Discovery of the Impairment

The group of parents, who were suddenly introduced to the idea that their children had physical problems, either because their impairments were discovered at birth or soon afterwards, or because their physical problems were caused by sudden serious illness, reported that they experienced a great deal of anxiety or intense feelings of shock, distress and confusion. Only one set of parents reported no stress at this time because their son was not seriously affected by his condition. Darren's father described his experiences:

It shattered us, he caused a lot of problems in one go. We were upset, crying, knocked down flat. It affected us in every way, home life, with the other two.

His wife added:

I'd never had an ill child before. I didn't know what to expect. While he was very ill I felt detached from it. It was as if I was in another room.

Eight sets of parents reported experiencing some difficulties in grasping the initial information given to them with, in some cases, a sense of detachment from the event. A further ten sets of parents described their early intense need for further information, for an explanation of what had happened to them and of what would happen in the future. Some parents spoke of asking the questions 'Why us? Why our child?', an apparent need for a basic explanation of the reason for their experience. In other cases, parents described a conscious need for more information about their children's physical problem, about how they might develop and about how they themselves should approach their new parenting task. As Paula's mother illustrates:

I wanted to know more, I wanted to know what I had to cope with.

James' mother said:

You need support from someone who knows, who can fill in the details as you go along.

She was not referring merely to information about cystic fibrosis as a medical condition but to the implications of the impairment for her son and for the ways in which she would have to attempt to meet his needs.

Two sets of parents reported a different experience. One of them has a son, Marcus who had been physically able before suffering a serious illness at the age of three which left him profoundly deaf. They also suffered intense distress at the time of his illness. They explained:

> *We just didn't know what day it was. I have never cried so much in all my life as I did during the first six months to one year. I couldn't handle it. No one told us anything. I just cried. I couldn't use the word `deaf'. It was like fostering someone else's child.*

The other set of parents have a five year old who was impaired after an intracranial aneurism. His mother explained:

> *You mourn the child he was.*

These parents shared with the others the anxiety and distress of discovering their sons' illness and subsequent impairments and the need for information about the possible outcome of the event, but they also experienced the added burden, having known their child ad fit and healthy, of grief and of getting to know them as people with impairments. Not only were their constructs of their parenting challenged but their existing constructs of their children were invalidated.

Hourd (1972) writes that in learning, there are times when an individual's progress is static, when there is; 'A necessary state of bewilderment' (p.37). It appears that many parents experience this state at the early stage, a major life event which challenges both their expectations and their existing knowledge. Hourd continues to say that this state can be very painful indeed:

> *We can feel like someone caught in revolving doors seeing the way back and the way forward, and yet not going one way or the other. But often these doors connect out different ways of knowing, and what seems like confusion and uncertainty is a movement in the process of clarification (p.37).*

The Adoption of a Present Time Perspective

All the parents seemed to experience similar processes when they first discovered their children's physical problems. The sudden discovery that their children were not as they expected, that there was something different about them, that they were impaired, clearly caused intense distress. Often, at the time of diagnosis, events were changing rapidly, giving parents little time to take in the information available to them. There were preoccupations, on the part of parents and professionals alike, with the hourly, daily or weekly progress of the children. In some cases, parents described changes in their time perspective. Jenny's parents said:

> *We knew within fifteen minutes of her birth. They told us everything; oesophageal atresia, no rectum, malformed bladder, one partially working kidney, the other absent, no vagina and a malformed lower spine. They said she had a milk intolerance and a limited life expectancy. We were told she wouldn't live after birth so we were given the choice of letting her die. I made the decision in my wife's absence. I said `No'. She stopped breathing once and they resuscitated her before we were informed. Time seemed to stand still. It didn't all sink in at first. It's a shock at first. Then you cry a lot.*

In many areas of life, people identify goals and adapt strategies and behaviours intended to attain them. They are set at one point in the future and behaviours carried out tin the present are expected to increase the probability of reaching them. Thus achievements are related to identifying and achieving goals both of which are set in future time. Jones (1988) suggests that, in our society, a future time perspective predominates. This is seen by people as linear and forward flowing and is strongly guided by perceptions of desirable goals set in the future. However, Jones argues that:

> *Goals localised in the distant future can affect present behaviour only if there is a temporal integration that makes the future continuous with the present, and internal causal attributions that recognise personal control in achieving outcomes (p.29).*

At the early stages of beginning to understand the implications of their children's differentness, these parents appear to have adopted a present time perspective. In this case, time consciousness is suspended and action occurs in the infinite present. Social time is functional, non-directional and present orientated. The experience of living minute by minute or day by day indicates the effort of continual survival. Present behaviour is assumed to be expressive of feelings now, and there are proximal goals to be achieved, such as the survival of the child. As parents' constructs are negated or challenged and events relating to their earliest experiences of caring for their child change rapidly and frequently they do not initially identify future goals. Elizabeth's' father described similar early experiences to those of Jenny's parents. He said:

She was fourteen weeks premature. There were two weeks in intensive care and she had an intro-ventricular haemorrhage, kidney failure, septicaemia, jaundice and respiratory distress syndrome. She almost died several times. For us, the first few weeks were about survival only.

Jones also indicates that, in our society, this future time perspective is a basic formulation for construal of events but that people need a blend of the best characteristics of both future and present time perspectives within an integrated functional whole. He warns that there is a danger that the present time perspective can be seen by others as:

..a deficiency of character and / or capacity, whereas the future time perspective has been presented simply as the `right' way to view the world (p.28).

Yet, in their recollections, those parents who experienced rapid changes in their children's health did seem to temporarily adopt a present time perspective, which may reflect not only the negation of their existing constructs but may also indicate a typical response to a rapidly shifting experience of uncertainty.

The Gradual Discovery of the Impairment

The ten sets of parents whose discovery of their children's physical problems came before professional acknowledgement, reported different experiences from the parents described above. They were spared the sudden shock of learning that their children were impaired and the intense distress and confusion accompanying sudden discovery. On the other hand, they experienced daily anxiety about their children's physical development. For some parents this process lasted for days, weeks, months or even years before they were able to gain professional acknowledgement, advice and treatment for their children. They experienced the stresses of daily unanswered questions and the quest for information which might confirm their fears. Hannah's mother described in detail the experience of attempting to find an explanation for her daughter's physical problems:

She was a prem baby, born six and a half weeks early. When she was born, despite her prematurity, they said she was very good. She was in the special care unit but she was only in an incubator for two days. We brought her home assuming that she was a normal little baby. At ten months, she had a funny rash which started to reappear and we began to get worried. It came and went and it was put down to a heat rash as it was summer time. After about two *weeks the rash started to come with fevers. That's when we really started to worry and went to the doctor. The paediatrician thought she'd had an infection which would clear up, but it didn't. She began to refuse to weight bear. We were referred back to the hospital but we still didn't get very far. We ended going weekly. They were still telling us it was an infection. At sixteen months we plucked up courage to say that we were not happy and wanted to see someone else. It was then suggested that it might be arthritis and we were given an appointment within two days. The consultant took one look at Hannah and said, `Yes, I know what it is'. We were six months with a poorly child. There were times when I thought she would just give up. We actually got to the stage we took photos of the rash because it came on in the evenings and she would see the doctor in the mornings. We tried to show them how bad it was. We didn't consider that we had a normal child by any means.*

Parents described their sense of relief at professional confirmation of their children's impairments. They also experienced anxiety and stress but it was seen to be related to their daily worries about their children's development and to the lack of professional acknowledgement. As they gleaned more information they were able to elaborate their fears and thus make a more convincing argument to the professionals concerned.

Realisation and Birth Order

The position of the children in their families was found to be important in the realisation process. The following table shows the relationship between the discovery of the impairment and birth order.

Table 4
The Discovery of the Impairment and the Position of the Child in the Family

Process of Discovery	Position in Family		Total
	First/Only	Subsequent Child	
Children diagnosed at birth	7	11	18
Children diagnosed later in childhood	4	10	14
Children whose impairments were discovered by parents before professional acknowledgement	3	8	11

Of the children in the sample, three were only children and two were twins, although in each case the other twin was able bodied. The research found that parents of single children had learned a new routine which, inside their families, was their only measure of parenting. As Elizabeth's father explained:

We've learned all our family life from her.

Another parent said:

To us it's a normal family life.

This suggests again that perceptions of parenting were based on the care of the disabled child; yet all the parents in the sample used an external measure of the differentness of their parenting through contracts with other parents or occasionally through direct involvement with the care of able bodied children. Elizabeth's mother described her experiences:

I often look after my friends' children. I realise now that looking after able bodied children is so easy because they can help themselves.

Another mother said:

I suppose life is different. To us it's a normal family life. We notice it with our nephews who are more vigorous than John.

Parents whose eldest children were physically impaired also found that they had no initial external measures of how their children, or their parenting, were different, but they described how their experience of parenting subsequent children helped them to gain internal measures. As a mother indicated:

If I'd had our son first, I'd have seen her problems more clearly. I was blind to it. I had no one to compare her with because she was my first child. He now emphasises her problems.

In some cases, parents took steps to create what they saw as an environment which is more like that of other families. Hannah's father said:

Having found out that it wasn't genetic we were definite that we'd have another child. We felt that it was important. It would have been a big reason not to have another one but we had to think more clearly about it. Other parents feel differently. We felt it justified having other children, as long as they were healthy, it would maintain as normal a pattern of life as possible and being normal children into the house.

These parents recognised that at first, their parenting was based solely upon meeting Hannah's needs. With the arrival of another child, they were able both to modify their perceptions of her degree of differentness and recognise the ways in which their parenting had been different.

The parents whose older children were physically able had already established their perceptions of parenting. They indicated that with the discovery of their children's impairments, they were faced with demands from two directions. The needs of their able bodied children continued, yet they had to establish an extra dimension to their parenting in order to cope with the new and unknown demands of caring for their impaired children. All of the parents who discovered their children's impairments suddenly, indicated that, during this early stage, the equilibrium of their family lives was disrupted. Darren's father said:

> *It affected us in every way, home life and with the other two. Everything was thrown into a massive pile in the middle of the floor and you had to sort out the pieces quickly because the rest of the family depends on you and you have to carry on as a mother and father. But ninety per cent of getting through is getting the routine right.*

Parents who discovered their children's impairments gradually also indicated that their other children played a part in the realisation process.

The Influence of People Outside the Family in the Process of Realisation

Parents indicated that they used external measures to assist them in the realisation process. Through comparison with both able bodied and impaired children and with the parenting they receive, they were able to begin to understand the implications. Andrea's mother described the steps she took to establish some meaning for her experience:

> *I knew of no one with eczema so I began the local support group. You can really relate to other women who say that they get desperate and that they could throw their child with excema out of the window. You can say, `Oh! I feel like that!' It makes you feel more normal. We've learned a lot from the support group. We now realise how lucky we are to have her, in comparison with others.*

Some parents described useful contacts with other physically impaired children and their parents, during visits to hospitals or clinics. Mandy's mother said:

> *It was at about six months that I realised that something was wrong. I was, of course, comparing with the elder daughter. I mentioned it at the prem baby clinic and they wouldn't commit themselves for a while. Then they decided she needed physiotherapy. She was just under a year then. It was when I was talking to another Mum at the centre and I asked her what was wrong with her child. She said it was cerebral palsy and it was very similar to what was wrong with Mandy so I asked the physio and she said `Yes'.*

Parents spoke of comparing their children with other impaired and able bodied children to help them to understand the nature and degree of their differentness. Tina has spina bifida and she is very dependent on her parents' care. After she was born, her mother established a mother and toddler group. She described how she persisted in attending despite her distress at coming into close contact with, 'normal babies'.

Parents indicated that professionals also had an important part to play in the realisation process. By imparting the information that their children are less than physically perfect, they contribute to the challenge to parents' existing constructs of childhood and of their emerging role as parents, but they were also seen as a primary source of vital information about the impairment, its likely progress and about how parents might meet their children's needs.

Roskies (1972) writes that a physically impaired person is both normal and abnormal, a member of a community yet different from other members. She argues that such a person has a duel identity and is, 'marginal between two cultures' (p.19). It seems that the realisation process involves parents in the establishment of an understanding of their children's marginality, of the nature and degree of their differentness from other children. All the parents in the sample appear to have used a number of sources to enable them to establish an understanding of their children's identity. They used the internal measure of comparison with their other children and the child's position in the family was found to be a factor in the process of establishing an understanding of the nature, degree and implications of his or her impairment. Brothers and sisters played an important role in this process but where parents had one child, they used other social relationships in their quest for a measure of their differentness. In most cases, parents said that they also used external measures in their contacts with other parents and children, both able bodied and impaired and with specialist professionals who were seen to play an important role in the realisation profess. The way in which parents first learn that, 'something is wrong' may vary according to the certainty with which professionals are able to identify the physical problem, but parents' realisation of their children's impairments is a dynamic process in which professionals continue to play a part.

Part 4
Appraisal Studies

The Delights of Learning to Apply the Life History Method to School Non-Attenders

DAVID BOWEN

*This account of the life history method vividly highlights the way in which understanding qualitative research can unexpectedly produce personal insights and self-learning for the practitioner-researcher and subjects alike. David Bowen describes how he went about creating a sample of non-school attenders and then followed through with fieldwork. Eventually he had twelve meetings with four subjects and three wrote their autobiographies. In Abraham Lincoln's words he made contact with 'the better angels of their nature'. The account combines rich data and personal experience with a celebration of the subjects' integrity - **Editors.***

Learning to Apply the Life History Method to School Non-Attenders

Much has been written, about children who do not go to school. They have been subjected to questionnaires (Eaton, 1979), been counted and placed in groups (Douglas and Ross, 1965), examined within their institutions (Rutter et al., 1979). Solutions to the problem of absenteeism have been proposed. Some were institutional (Grunsell, 1978), some organisational and administrative (Galloway, 1976) and others societal (Starr, 1981).

The Appeal of the Life History Method

The method seemed appropriate because it allowed the main people involved to speak for themselves. It was attractive to me because it would make use of some of the skills I had learned and used as a practising social worker. However, the move from an understanding of the theory of life history to its application remained a daunting one.

Unlike many other sociological research methods, life history depends on the researcher's ability to establish a rapport with a number of subjects over a lengthy period. Data is gathered through unstructured interviews. The quality of the material obtained must be affected by the researcher's skill at probing and listening. Life history is an ad hoc method in that, with no notice, the subject may turn to different matters in the interview from those originally intended and the researcher must decide at the time what to do about that. It would have been most unfortunate had the research been designed around the method only for me to discover that I was unable to use it. I tested that in two ways.

Its Provisional Application

First, I approached a local education authority close to Cranfield and asked to be given the names, details, and addresses of a number of young people whose attendance at school was insufficiently poor to warrant juvenile court proceedings.

No further help was asked from the authority. I preferred to make unheralded calls as a student undertaking a project on what pupils thought about school. The new role was concerning. In the past (as a social worker) I had always had a reason which gave a comprehensible justification for my calling. In the student role I arrived, as it were, with empty hands outstretched, asking for help. I need not have feared. People were very kind and welcomed an interest even though I kept coming back.

My second way of testing the life history method was even less formal, and happened by chance. I had been using the facilities of a local leisure centre one evening a week, and had noticed a group of young people, mostly boys aged from about 14-16, there. The group was not always made up of the same people, but there was a constant nucleus. From observation and eavesdropping all the youngsters seemed to be generally disaffected with school and ostensibly bored with their lives. It seemed likely that, if I were to use the life history method in the research proper, I would be working with people holding similar attitudes. I fell into conversation with the group at the leisure centre. I found that they were quite happy to talk, that I could lead the conversation into paths in which I had an interest and that I was having practice in remembering and then recalling what had been said. I met the group for several weeks, on a regular evening.

Subsequently the families I visited were intrigued by my interest which made them and their stories feel important. There was no unwillingness to reveal the life history, even though time did not permit the full recording of it. One girl, despite a long history of refusal to attend school on a regular basis or to make any commitment to 'educational activity', readily wrote of her own experiences. Similarly, the group at the leisure centre showed no inhibition in discussing their experiences of school and their opinion of it. Although their views were not positive, they were expressed with a seriousness and degree of restraint which was different from their general conversation. This centred round their fanciful boastings of sexual exploits and activities in petty crime.

Lessons Learnt

In these trials, I was gaining skills in what might be called fieldcraft and confidence in using the method. The subjects received in return an overt interest in them as people. One boy of limited ability and short concentration span was 'recruited' by me as a 'research assistant' and paid small sums for his help and cooperation.

I gained considerable confidence from what can be loosely described as these two pilot studies. Most people were happy to give help when it was requested. Not one of the families I called on rejected my approach and some put themselves out quite considerably to accommodate my calling. One mother baked cakes when I was to call.

Through these visits and group discussions I learned several things which were critical to the success of the subsequent research. First, the life history method was a perfectly valid research instrument for the project in hand in that it revealed attitudes to education in general, and school in particular, and allowed comparison to be made with other influences on young people's lives. Second, young people could be encouraged and were quite prepared to reveal themselves through their own stories. Also as I was gathering information from which to draw conclusions, they were being valued and were learning about themselves. Less happily, I realised my inability to recall the content of interviews and therefore notetaking, or tape-recording, would be necessary. Finally, I realised that the process of gathering data was fun and this would help me maintain my commitment to the research.

Establishing a Sample: The Retrospective Option

The next stage in applying the life history method was to find the subjects for the full research project. The nature of my employment gave me both advantages and disadvantages in that whilst I was aware of all the children and young people in the county currently in care for educational reasons I had decided to bring each one before the court. I had met most of them, and our relationships had been authoritarian. These things combined to convince me that it would not be appropriate to seek their involvement in the research. The next possible group was those in care in another authority but distance was the major obstacle there and I knew that the life history method would require my visiting regularly and frequently.

It seemed more appropriate to concentrate on those who had completed the education/care process in the Local Authority or the county in which I worked. Their stories could give a retrospective picture, and enable me to understand the effect of the intervention on their lives as I would have had no involvement in their being made subject to care orders and access would be a straightforward matter. Descent into the basement at County Hall seemed called for but I was unprepared for the difficulties I was to face. The record storage system was in chaos. Archive cases of dead files were piled, with virtually no order, from floor to ceiling. I was compelled to search through dozens of boxes of files, most of which contained nothing of relevance, though much of interest. In that way I found records relating to fifteen people who had been made the subjects of care orders because they had not gone to school regularly, but were now over the age for care. The quality of the records was very poor, some were single page records.

Using the scanty records available, I wrote to the last address given for each of the fifteen. In the letters I adopted the student role which had been used successfully earlier and emphasised I was seeking confidential help. The letters evinced no response, other than two being returned by the Post Office and marked not known. I then visited each address. From these calls I finally found and spoke to four people who all agreed to be part of the research. It is their life stories which made up the core of the research.

Life Histories: Making the Most of the Opportunity for Self-Reflection

In my first meeting with each of the four whom I had found, I explained that I was undertaking a research project in which I wanted to hear the stories of people who had completed their education but had experienced difficulties in it. It was empha-sised that other researchers had considered the opinions of teachers and parents, but I was interested in the 'consumer's' view. I explained that I would be asking them to tell me their life history: that it would be very time consuming and might open up painful memories. It was clear from the start that I would make repeated calls and that this would interrupt their normal lives. All agreed readily.

In fact I had about 12 meetings with each subject, on a weekly basis although there were interruptions. At first I took notes during the conversations. After the first three or four meetings, when confidence had been won, I suggested tape-recording our discussions. Again there was no demur. When introducing the recorder, we played with it at first, allowing the subjects to hear their own voices and spending the early part of the interview in less serious talk. There was no apparent inhibition in the interviews caused by the tape-recorder: eight or nine hours of recording was done with each.

For three of the four subjects, a further stage followed. From the initial notes and the tape-recordings, I prepared an outline of an autobiography. This I presented to the subjects and asked that they write their own stories. After the initial shock that anyone would either want such a manuscript, or would think that it could be done, they agreed. I provided note books and encouragement through continued visits. In these I did not criticise the content of what had been written so far, but praised the effort made, underlined the importance of what was being done and tried to maintain the enthusiasm.

The results of the writing exercise were very encouraging. Diana presented me with over five and a half thousand words of autobiography . She made the time to write that while looking after her home, her boyfriend, her sister and her baby. Kenny her younger brother, produced over twelve thousand words. Althea, whose intellectual ability is patently lower than either of the others, wrote almost as much as Diana. These were three young people who had shown no interest in education while at school, had actively tried to avoid it, had made no attempt to renew their educational experience since leaving school, yet they willingly provided lengthy pieces of work. I doubt if any of them had written much more than a postcard since teachers stopped demanding it of them. Not always grammatically correct, properly punctuated or spelled, what I was given was lucid and alive.

The content was exciting, too, but reading the life stories as a piece showed the feelings, thoughts and attitudes of the writers in a way that I do not think I could have found by talking.

In the analysis of the written material, I abstracted from each autobiography quotations and recorded them on cards according to their topics. On the same cards I noted quotations from the tape-recorded interviews with all four subjects and from the notes I had made during our initial meetings. These cards were then sorted into linked themes. Through the subjects' eyes and in their own words, it was possible to see the instability of their homes and social life, the lack of interest their parents showed in education and the attempts they made to overcome absence from school. For the subjects of this research, the intervention of 'the authorities' had little effect.

All four had been placed in the care of the Local Authority because they had not gone to school regularly. In care they were moved like pieces on a chess board, with little thought for their education. Their lack of involvement in the process of care is striking. The outcome is saddening. Theirs are stories of failure. They failed to appreciate their own worth. Authorities failed to recognise their talents and so did nothing to capitalise on them. Three of the four subjects took their bodies to school while in care. None of them took their minds. They were not educated, despite the ostensible reason for their being in care: they were exposed to schooling.

It would be dishonest to maintain that I did not grow fond of my research subjects over the months we worked together. Their generosity of time, effort and spirit was amazing. They asked little of me, but gave a great deal of themselves. My gratitude to them is immeasurable. The conclusions were mine but the work was theirs.

Applying the Panel Studies Method to Professionals' Assessments of Clients' Needs

MIKE CARPENTER

Using a panel study the author explores ways in which lay citizens about to become 'clients', as well as existing 'clients' are initially allocated services and resources. The study illustrates a distinct advantage of this method after the panel has been set up, namely its efficiency in gathering a lot of basic data. The main finding, is that the type of Social Services assessed as suitable for clients will largely be determined by the perceptions of the agency making the assessment - is a matter of considerable importance, as everyone is a potential client! Going beyond this finding the data also shows the different perceptions which social workers, home helps, occupational therapists, social work assistants, day / residential staff have of their own jobs - Editors.

Setting Up the Panel Study

This panel study's exercise helped me to examine the ways in which workers from different professional backgrounds construed information about 80 potential Social Services clients whose details were outlined on referral forms. It attempts to examine whether referral decisions are uniformly accurate as perceived by different professionals provided with exactly the same basic information. The panel study was designed to gain some indication of how staff are influenced by referral information, and how, if at all, the more direct and obvious pre-selection by referral agents would be challenged. The information contained in the referrals was copied from original referral data. For the purpose of the panel study referrals were stripped of all identifying data and the documentation issued was limited to name, address, date of birth, general practitioner, and *the wording contained on the original referral itself.*

The panel process involved drawing together eight representatives from a single profession, and requesting each of them to consider a batch of ten referrals and nominally allocate them to a particular service or discipline. The exercise was then repeated using a second batch of ten referrals so that effectively two opinions were gained on each of the 80 cases. The process was repeated with five professional groups, namely social workers, home help organisers, occupational therapists, day/ residential staff and assistant social workers.

All the panels were set up on the same day in order to minimise, if not obviate totally, the opportunity for intercommunication between panel members. The only pre-amble to the panel exercise was a letter that went to each person selected indicating that they had been invited to take part in an exercise related to community care needs of the elderly. The panel members, when convened, were invited to undertake the exercise of allocating the cases with the minimum of explanation.

Each member involved in the exercise was asked to answer one question only with the first batch of ten cases. This required them to nominate the professional to whom the case should be allocated. The first batch was then withdrawn, and the panel members were allocated the second batch of ten referrals and asked to repeat the exercise. The process having been repeated, three supplementary questions were posed:

1. Why did they make the choice they did?
2. Was there any additional information they would normally require prior to allocation?
3. What would be the effect on their allocation decision of the client having had previous contact with the agency?

This piece concentrates on the answers to the first question.

The Views of the Social Workers

The social work group were challenging in that they often had difficulty in nominating an individual worker to a case as was requested of them, and asked if dual allocation was admissible. But when questioned about 'normal' practice they confirmed that single allocation was most common at the outset and then they agreed to follow established practice. The group also indicated that in this exercise they found the referral data very limited, because it was usually devoid of 'vital data' about the *emotional* impact of problems, instead it concentrated more on practical problem areas and conditions. For example, the case of Mrs E was referred for home help because of trouble with her back. The referral came from her sister, who confirmed that the general practitioner had indicated that the condition was degenerative. The social worker in the exercise asked why the sister had not been asked what Mrs E's reaction had been to the general practitioner's prognosis, whether she was aware of the referral, whether the client lived alone and, indeed, the extent of her physical limitations.

The second issue, about the client's awareness of the referral, features in many of the observations made by different professionals. This is an important matter in that relatives, often well-meaning, seek help for, or action on behalf of, a third party without having discussed the matter with them.

In their response the social workers also expressed the need for more background information about both an overall assessment and the individual elderly person. There were a number of examples of this including:

Mrs L seemed an 'obvious' home help referral, but her heart condition prompted the social worker to argue that a full assessment of reaction to physical problems should be undertaken.

The written referral stated 'Mrs G, discharged after hernia repair, husband can cope, but hospital staff feel follow-up required to provide help in home'. The social worker in this case felt that although the referral did state that help in the home might be necessary, the wording of the document, especially the indication that `husband can cope', warranted follow-up and further investigation.

The social workers found it impossible to answer whether or not a case should be allocated back to any previous worker and I believe this was a much to do with the incomplete information as the complexity of the cases, or the quality of social workers' decisions.

The Views of the Home Helps

It was noticeable in the home helps' panel responses how clearly they perceived the problems, and how comfortable they were about nominating a worker. It remains a matter of debate whether this finding is welcome (i.e. clear assessments) or disturbing (too simple 'solutions' to complete problems). Their judgements strictly followed the wording of referrals. This saw a situation as 'specifically' requiring help in the home, or 'specifically' requiring help with shopping. They seem to have a capacity to identify a problem very finitely and, on that basis, to prescribe answers to the situations. There were many examples including: Mrs I, who was referred by the occupational therapist from the hospital. The referral simply said: 'Osteo-arthritis, grossly overweight, hypertension'. The home help organiser's allocation was home help. The rationale behind the decision is worth recording in full:

Home help - with osteo-arthritis and grossly overweight it would be impossible for her to do housework or shopping. Occupational therapist referred her so presume she has enough aids. No additional information required.

In their responses this home help group frequently speculated about other possible problems that might exist, but seemed happy to accept the initial responsibility for a case, claiming that they would seek the help of colleagues if required. Many of the replies cast doubts on their awareness of clients' emotional need, revealing their task-based approach to work.

Where the home help organisers suggested that social work help would be required, it was often because a problem was identified which they felt might be time-consuming. Mr A was a good example, referred as needing help with financial problems. The home help organiser allocated this case to a social worker, the rationale being: 'Social worker will have more time to deal with past debts and home help once started will keep an eye on the situation'. It seems as if home help organisers almost regarded a request for help as an instruction as there was evidence of very literal translation of the information contained in referrals. In all but a very few cases they indicated that they would not be influenced by the fact that the case was previously known to the department, certainly not to the extent of changing their mind about the nominated worker.

The Views of the Occupational Therapists

Like the home help organisers, the occupational therapists were very much led and directed by the specific wording on the referral. Physical problems were ascertained as appropriate for intervention by an occupational therapist. Practical problems were divided into two categories - firstly, those inside the home (where home help was presumed to be the right response), and secondly, those outside the home (related to care of garden and so on) where assistant social workers, occupational therapy aids, home help aids, or one of the voluntary organisations were considered appropriate.

The occupational therapists, unlike their home help colleagues, nominated a social worker when the referral was not specific, their logic being that the social worker was the best person to undertake a full assessment. This occurred in the case of Mrs B, who was referred by her neighbour. The following is the wording of the written assessment.

Mrs B is a widow, is very depressed, lives alone. Has two brothers but no contact. Neighbour states that she had recently seen her general practitioner but is unaware of results. Could assessment be made of what help can be given? Mrs B is very isolated, although neighbours do offer support when around. She is putting some strain on them and she keeps on about dying and informing them what to do if they find her dead.

In general terms the occupational therapists were led by the direct referral request but they also saw value in assessments which they regarded as being the prerogative of social workers. They made much of the need to contact their opposite numbers in the health authority whether working in hospitals or in the community in order to establish whether there is any previous history on the client.

The Views of the Day/Residential Staff

The first choice of worker by this group followed a very similar pattern to the previous groups. The most interesting point of divergence was that frequently a second worker was indicated and, in many cases, this was either a health visitor, a district nurse or a general practitioner. Mrs A was a case in point. This was a lady whose referral was: 'A chronic condition producing vomiting'. The home help organisers saw this as requiring their help, whilst the day and residential staff agreed with the occupational therapists that a social worker assessment was required. The day and residential staff would make it a joint assessment with a general practitioner. It would seem that this group were particularly conscious of the medical implications of some of the conditions outlined in the referrals probably reflecting their residential and semi-residential experiences with people needing considerable medical, as well as social, support.

The other interesting feature was that, if in doubt, the day and residential staff, as with the earlier occupational therapist group, regarded it as being the prerogative of the social worker to undertake a full assessment of the individual. This was highlighted in the case of Mrs M, who was referred to a social worker in the panel study exercise as follows: 'Discharged from hospital last week. Had gynaecological operation - needs bath aids (both seat and grab rail)'.

The rationale behind their decisions was not always easy to follow, but it would seem that the possible emotional impact of any given situation prompted day and residential staff to feel that a social worker should at least make the initial assessment.

In terms of additional information required, this group was less demanding, and in the few cases where it was requested it was related to medical facts, and the financial and physical circumstances of the individuals concerned.

The Views of the Assistant Social Workers

The assistant social workers followed a familiar pattern and allocated very much in accord with the specific details on the referral. Again, as with the previous two groups, they saw a role for more social work assessments of the overall situation, although often to be conducted in tandem with some other practical service. This approach was in evidence with Mrs L, who was referred by her son: 'Mrs L suffers from a heart condition. Needs help with cleaning'.

The assistant social workers saw this as requiring both a social worker assessment to ascertain to what degree her heart condition affected her way of life, and the home help organiser for cleaning/shopping.

As a group the assistant social workers quite often prescribed a second service, anticipating the possible need for it, and using it as some form of insurance.

Summary Observations of the Panel Study Exercise

The results of the panel study proved to be statistically significant in that each profession allocated referrals to themselves more often than was the average incidence of allocation by other professionals. In other words an initial interpretation of need based on the same data can be significantly different from one profession to another and this may be a major problem. In turn this serves to highlight the need to concentrate on the referral process, and be more aware of the different range of services offered by various professionals.

The overall distribution of results indicates that each profession is more likely to regard its own service as the appropriate response than any of the others. For example in respect of social workers I discovered that generally they received 22% of all referrals whereas they referred a higher percentage, 30% to themselves. The same was true for the other occupational groups. The respective figures for these groups was as follows: occupational therapists, 32% generally and 49% to themselves; Home Help organisers 35% generally and 56% to themselves; assistant social workers 4% and 8% ; and finally for residential/ day staff the figures were 8% and 13%. In other words for each profession the proportion of 'self-referrals' is contrasted with the average allocation to that profession. For example, the general tendency to refer to home help organisers and occupation therapists is greatly exaggerated by the home help organisers and occupational therapists themselves. The significance of this result lies in the fact that it tends to support the hypothesis, presented earlier, that professionals will tend to 'screen' for the service *they* provide.

I conclude that there is a strong likelihood that the prospective client will eventually receive *either* the service requested - when one is specifically mentioned in the referral - *or* the service provided by the worker to whom the duty desk makes the initial allocation. Given that there are no strong controls on this initial allocation - little in the way of filtering goes on - it is not unreasonable to conclude that that important decision largely determines what the outcome of assessment will be. Indeed, whether this system really merits the name 'assessment' is another question. In looking at alternative and fairer assessment methods then, this panel study has highlighted the need for a form of inter-disciplinary assessment which eliminates, or at least substantially reduces, the bias of single agency assessments.

Recognising Elderly Abuse

BARBARA MALLON

*Investigative studies can take the form of developing a definition and thereby what could be the appropriate responses. Abuse, for example, occurs as child abuse, spouse abuse and elderly abuse yet are they really so similar? If they differ is that because of emotional and economic ties or because of legal and medical concerns? Most significantly of all how do practitioners in contact with abuser and abused define what is happening? Barbara Mallon studied Social Services' staff to seek their understanding of elderly abuse. She then considered its prevalence, its patterns and its causes. Those abused are mostly women either by their spouse or by their off-spring. As Mallon writes, evidence like this 'challenges cherished beliefs about family life'. Her method was a careful sifting and sorting of information from staff. The skill was to locate potentially shocking findings in simple descriptive statistics - **Editors.**

Although there has been an increasing number of research projects there is still no universally accepted definition of what constitutes elder abuse. This raises various problems for researchers. In an attempt to clarify how Social Services staff recognise and deal with cases of elder abuse it was vital to establish their understanding of elder abuse. It was hoped that in using the research methods which I did, that I would encourage staff to explore their own feelings, understanding and interests in the subject. Respondents in a study carried out by Rowlings (1981) suggested that emotional abuse is more common than physical injury. However, most British research into elder abuse has focused on incidents of physical abuse (Hocking and Eastman, 1984; Pritchard, 1989), making comparisons between research findings difficult. This research identified emotional abuse as the most frequent type of abuse, followed by physical abuse.

According to Mildenberger and Wessman (1986) determining the most common type of abuse is difficult. There are various assumptions that there are parallel relationships between child abuse, spouse abuse, and elder abuse which according to Hotaling, Finkelhor, Kirkpatrick and Straus (1988) may be untrue.

Hotaling et al. (1988) comment that what is not sufficiently recognised is that some cases of elder abuse is spouse abuse which has been going on in a relationship for years and can in some situations intensify as the couple age. Fieldworkers have identified cases of spouse abuse continued into old age. In these cases they also come up against a reluctance on the part of the person being abused to take any steps to rectify the situation, frequently accepting that the abuse would continue and intervention was not going to help. It is possible that people who have been abused over a period of time become caught in the trap of learnt helplessness.

Elderly people unlike children, are seen as having more social, psychological and economic independence and as such are seen as having the choice about whether or not they remain in an abusing and/or neglectful situation. This was commented on by Hotaling et al. (1988) as well as the fieldworkers in this research. But often the elderly person may be connected to the abuser by their ties of emotional allegiance and perhaps economic dependence. Without appropriate support and information adults may be left trapped in situations which for numerous reasons they are unable to escape.

Elder abuse is often compared and contrasted with child abuse because the relationship between the caretaker and the elderly person is often thought to have the characteristics of a parent - child relationship in the extreme dependency of the elderly person. Also child abuse having been first identified by professionals is within their sphere of knowledge and understanding whereas, professionals have more limited contact with adults involved in spouse abuse. The procedures for involvement with child abuse and more lately elder abuse have been medicalised by health professionals. Admittedly in some areas elder abuse shares some similarities with child abuse. However, children do not have a legal responsibility for their parents. There is also a very different structural relationship between adult children and parents.

Breckman and Adelman (1988) would argue that moving away from a child abuse analogy and placing elder abuse within a domestic violence perspective would make it easier to compare elder abuse with spouse abuse. They are supported in their findings by Pillemer and Finkelhor (1988) who also hold that a considerable proportion of elder abuse is spouse abuse. Furthermore it is possible that by using a spouse abuse analogy professionals and society cease to adopt ageist attitudes and recognise that many elderly people are relatively independent responsible adults. Unfortunately Breckman and Adelman (1988) do not address the problem from the perspective of physically or mentally dependent adults, although they do say that elder abuse is not usually compared with spouse abuse due to the conceptualisation of elder abuse as a problem of caregiving. Steinmetz and Anderson (1983) clarify this further when they say that:

> *...the dynamics in an elder abuse situation is presumed to be that of an overburdened caregiver who is unprepared for the stress of having to care for a relative and who, in frustration, lashes out at the elderly person.*

Parallels in child abuse and elder abuse are fundamentally flawed. Fieldworkers in this research highlighted some of these flaws:

1. Elderly people have choice.
2. There are no clear statutory laws for intervention.
3. Adult children have no legal responsibility to care for their parents (this responsibility which was part of the Poor Law was removed with the introduction of the National Assistance Act 1948).
4. Not all elderly people live with adult children.
5. Not all abusers are adult children.
6. In some of the cases identified it was the carer who was abused by dependent elderly person.

Abuse is understood best according to Ferguson and Beck (1983) when viewed as a symptom of family dysfunction caused by a variety of factors. But as this research has indicated elderly people are frequently assessed independently of their family dynamics.

In this study Social Services' staff attempted to define their understanding of abuse of elderly people. This was at three levels. First, they defined abuse in terms of cases. Secondly, staff explained their own understanding of abuse. Thirdly, they commented on a checklist of possible types of abuse which I had devised. They produced a varied selection of definitions of abuse with varying similarities.

Not all staff agreed on what constituted abuse. Of staff, 83% included physical abuse within their definition, whilst 63% mentioned emotional abuse, 29% mentioned neglect, however, only 3% mentioned financial abuse.

The cases identified by staff did not totally reflect the definitions of elder abuse outlined by staff. Senior social workers and fieldworkers identified a total of 133 cases of abuse of which: 53 percent of the cases were of emotional abuse, 51 percent of cases were classified as physical abuse, 17 percent of cases were defined as financial abuse and only 11 percent of cases were identified as neglect of the elderly person. Some cases contained more than one type of abuse against the elderly person. The most frequent types of abuse against an elderly person were those classified under active abuse. These included shouting, yelling, swearing, as well as, beating, hitting, and slapping the elderly person. However, staff did not always identify elements of emotional abuse or distress within physical abuse cases, it would appear that staff had not always acknowledged that to be physically abused can be emotionally distressing for the person being abused.

One of the major problems facing professionals working with elder abuse cases is in recognising that abuse is happening. Social Services' staffs' ability to recognise elder abuse relied on their own instincts to alert them to the fact that something was wrong and this was dependent on the experience and knowledge of individual workers:

> *The recognition of elder abuse is for the most part still at the gross physical level though more subtle features such as finger marks due to harsh gripping are now being recognised (Bennett, 1990).*

How staff actually recognised abuse was varied. In a small number of cases the worker was told by the elderly person that they were being abused. Generally, the abuse was recognised over a period of time. Only two cases were identified as abuse cases at the point of referral. So detecting abuse and neglect is frequently a matter of... 'putting all the pieces together and coming up with a definite diagnoses' (Quinn and Tomita, 1986). One point which was clearly emphasised in this research was that cases of elder abuse were not defined as such when they were initially referred. This could be for various reasons including the possibility that the referrer was not aware of the abuse or was not prepared to voice their concerns:

> *A not uncommon complaint from social workers is that referrals on families caring for a dependent elderly person come `too late' when attitudes and patterns of behaviour have become settled and the point of desperation has been reached on one or both sides (Rowlings, 1981).*

Detecting abuse is partly dependent on the worker realising that abuse and neglect exists and being aware of the different types. It may be that abuse goes unrecognised for several reasons, firstly, that the agencies do not support practitioners who try to work with abuse. There was certainly strong evidence in this research that fieldworkers were not supported in their work with elder abuse cases. All DCOs and unqualified staff claimed to report all cases of abuse to their senior social worker. Whereas, social workers admitted to have only reported 27 % of the abuse cases identified in this study. However, the cases mentioned by senior social workers did not reflect the fieldworkers' claims.

Seventy per cent of seniors claimed DCOs had no abuse cases and 30% claimed social work assistants had no abuse cases. Not surprisingly 40 percent of fieldworkers admitted to receiving no advice and/or recommendation from seniors in relation to abuse cases. This could be because all those involved do not recognise the seriousness of what they are dealing with. Secondly, it is possible: '...that workers are so busy trying to solve the problem that they do not recognise the cause or are too concerned about the problem to worry about the cause' (Quinn and Tomita, 1986). If professionals are not able to recognise abuse or are unwilling for whatever reasons to report cases of abuse they can become part of the collusion.

The extent of stress and strain experienced by the carer is not necessarily a clear indicator of abuse. As has been clearly identified, stress and stress alone does not lead all carers to abuse their dependent elderly relatives. The results of Eastman's Community Care survey (1984) indicated that stress was considered to be the overriding factor causing relatives to abuse.

The process of eliciting information from the staff interviewed also involved asking for some information about the possible causes of abuse as well as identifying the possible characteristics of the abuser and abused. Staff commented on the role of carers and the possible stress and strains carers are under. Some staff underlined the fact that the role of carers in caring for elderly people is one of vital importance, especially with the increasing pressure on professionals to think in terms of community care. To move towards a clearer understanding of what leads to elder abuse I felt professionals needed to increase their understanding of the role of carers and that carers' need to play a more active role in communicating with professionals. As a high percentage of elder abuse is carried out by a family member professionals cannot afford to ignore carers.

Establishing possible causes of abuse in the cases identified by seniors and fieldworkers was not always easy. The fieldworkers' responses were often mixed. Senior social workers identified stress and the health of the elderly person as the most frequent cause of the abuse. In some cases there was more than one cause identified. Some fieldworkers identified that victims of abuse are intimidated by their abusers and are afraid to leave the situation. This was highlighted as a problem of intervention by Hotaling and Finkelhor et al. (1988). Another problem for workers is in ascertaining the existence of abuse because victims and families do not readily admit to it. The acknowledgement of carers of:

> *...violent feelings towards one's parents are perhaps less easy to acknowledge than those against one's children where publicity has done much to make people aware of the potential for abuse (Rowlings, 1981).*

Rowlings goes on to state that for this reason: '...the social worker may have to take the initiative in exploring the possibility of abuse'. Ten years on, professionals are slowly beginning to recognise the possibility of elder abuse and to take the initiative. Unfortunately most workers are still having to work without guidelines, procedures or training. There is still a great deal of resistance to the recognition of abuse by professionals as it challenges cherished beliefs about family life.

The signs and symptoms identified by fieldwork staff are unlikely to be found in isolation. Signs and symptoms are often identified in clusters. Fieldworkers identified the signs and symptoms which they had experienced or those they would expect to find. With the exception of physical signs mentioned by 80% of fieldworkers, changes in attitude and changes in character of the elderly person were mentioned by 36% of staff. Staff were quite divided on the possible signs and symptoms to be aware of. A lot of staff relied on their own intuition. Staff also mentioned that they would rely on picking up the signs and/or symptoms of abuse from the elderly person, but admitted that the elderly person may not want to acknowledge the abuse. Some researchers, including Sengstock and Hwalek (1987), found that elderly people were reluctant to report the abuse for a variety of reasons. Basically workers appeared unsure of the types of signs and symptoms which might alert them to elder abuse cases. Workers need to be able to relate their experiences of elder abuse cases to a framework which would enable them to assimilate the information gained from one category of abuse cases into recognising the signs and symptoms in other abuse cases.

Social Services' staff identified a family member as the most frequent abuser of an elderly relative which should be of no surprise in view of the fact that most elderly people dependent on care are cared for by a family member. Of the 133 cases identified by Social Services' staff a total of 136 elderly people were being abused. There were 52 (38%) cases of abuse by a spouse and 53 (39%) cases of abuse by an adult child. Seventy eight percent of those identified by staff as being abused were female. Of these 33% were mothers abused by an adult child and 30% were wives abused by their husbands. Seventy five per cent of the elderly people identified as being abused lived with someone, of which 41% lived with a spouse and 26% lived with an adult child. So at least 65% of elderly people did not live with an adult child, yet the likelihood of being abused by an adult child is slightly more frequent than being abused by a spouse. This could reflect the possible reluctance on the part of professionals to identify the elderly person as either the carer or the possibility of the carer being the one who is abused.

The average age for the women being abused was 82 years and the men were on average 79 years. The most common health problem was dementia followed by general frailty. In 53 per cent of the fieldworkers' cases the person being abused was the one identified as the client, although 33 per cent of staff did acknowledge that where possible they worked with other family members as well.

There was a total of 149 persons identified as abusers of which eight were not related to the family member. Although some elderly people were abused by more than one person, not all abusers were carers. Fourteen elderly carers were being abused by the person they were caring for. The percentage of carers being abused by the elderly dependent is quite small in comparison to the number of elderly people who were identified by seniors and fieldworkers as being abused. Half the carers interviewed in this research were being abused by the person they cared for.

Part Five
Innovation Studies

Participative Research Possibilities: Windows on Collective Working

ALAN STANTON

Using only a selection of quotations this unusual and provocative piece highlights the way in which the Delphi model[1] of research ('a paper dialogue') was applied and presented. The replies collected using this model provide a summary commentary on different groups' experiences of collective working. This piece records the third stage of the author's research, the earlier two involved participant observation at one project, and later preliminary and full visits and interviews at several collaborative and collective teams. Some of the groups were 'genuine' collectives; formally non-hierarchical, with team decision-making, equal pay, and substantial sharing or rotation of work. Others were moving in this direction, towards what the author has described as 'collaborative team working'.[2] Although the researchers ambitious aim of facilitating an extensive discussion and debate among the teams taking part was not realised, edited material was circulated to all the participating groups and the questionnaire succeeded in unlocking and accessing a deluge of material (over 200 pages of edited summaries).

*The approach of only presenting quotations is to illustrate and highlight specific points, provoke discussion and, generally, inform, as well as amuse. In presenting full quotations as 'voices', the research attempts dialogical work between researcher and respondents. The author has not discounted whatever cannot 'be counted', sometimes a flaw of 'conventional' research. Overall the distinctive feature of this piece of research is that the author gave the respondents a certain freedom (and responsibility) to select and reject which of the questions from a 20 page questionnaire were most important to them. In this sense the thematic headings which follow, reflect both their main concerns, and the researcher's belief in participative research between researcher and respondents.[3] - **Editors.** (Notes based on Alan Stanton's own account).*

Democracy, Authority and Decision-Making

Questions

1. Where does authority lie in your agency/group?
2. Please describe your decision-making.
3. Are you satisfied with the efficiency and effectiveness of your decision-making? What changes have you tried out?
4. How informed are your decisions? Is information properly passed round (for instance, to part-time workers)?
5. Please describe your use of meetings.
6. Is there a formal or informal hierarchy? (For example, with 'heavy' and 'light' votes?)
7. Do you have a co-ordinator or chairperson? How does this operate?
8. Is there a conflict between working collectively and the functions of your agency?
9. How are these issues related to your size?
10. How do you plan ahead?

Quotations

We don't vote. Everybody speaks their mind. If one of the more experienced people strongly disagrees with what's going through, and says it with sufficient force and panic, then we'll sit on it for a week.

Some groups you don't talk about leaders. It's not supposed to happen. I think we would say that different people become leaders at different times.

It really is easier to run a hierarchical system. You don't carry so much responsibility. You push the crap upwards. But that's not what we're about. I feel it very heavily...taking responsibility for other people's cases.

All I want to do is my job, and they want me to make decisions.

They see me as just the typist and frankly, some of them don't think I've got the brains to cast my vote.

The new people weren't around when we were struggling to establish ourselves. W does have a heavy vote. But he has the right to guard the things he fought for.

A group of people aren't often able to make a difficult decision, or an adventurous decision. And a group of people can't acquire the detailed experience in sufficient areas to make as good a decision as an individual could.

Our place talks about collective responsibility and group decisions because we think it's the only efficient way of working with the kids we've got. The real inefficiencies of it are nothing in comparison with the inefficiencies of a hierarchical system. In that kind of set-up the leader goes around talking about whether you've got inner authority or not. The reason he's the one with the inner authority is that he's the one with all the power. The kids know that: they aren't fools.

...meetings which go round in circles, are not positive and don't arrive at a decision

Pay and Conditions

Questions

1. Please describe your salary structure. How much are you paid?
2. And are there non-cash benefits?
3. What is your policy on differentials and parity? Do you pay according to need?
4. What is your experience of altering the pay structure? And with what results?
5. What hours do you work? Has this changed, and why?
6. Please comment on your working conditions. How do you allocate space and facilities within your workplace?
7. Do you have paid/unpaid volunteers? Please comment.

Quotations

We should have everyone the same. But the Union has locked us into graded pay scales.

In the end it's just a job. It's ten times better than anything else I could get. And there are three million unemployed out there.

It's hard enough trying to get people to accept group responsibility. If we had wage differentials people would have the natural temptation to say: I'm on a couple of thousand less than so-and-so so what difference does the collective make?

Even the jokes people used to make. 'Here he comes. The part-timer who doesn't do reception any more'. You begin to feel that you really are a different person; that you aren't a peer. You are also aware of the fact that people are working 70 hours a week. In fact, I was doing much more than that, part-time hours. But there was this feeling that this was 'Gentleman Jim'.

There was a short pay scale, and you could choose what you needed. Nobody was supposed to discuss what you'd chosen. But somehow they made me feel guilty.

Take reception. It can be the heaviest job in the office. Why should the lowest paid person do it while I sit next door? Anyway, receptionists don't receive anybody. They're Local Authority bouncers.

*It's psychologically middle class. This is advanced middle class.
This is the socialist middle class, where obviously, they've outgrown
mere things like money. It's being wonderful, and therefore loved,
and therefore powerful.*

Hiring, Leaving and Firing

Questions

1. What procedures do you use for selecting new people?
2. Are they effective?
3. What qualifications, skills, or experience do you look for?
4. How do you communicate your expectations to applicants?
5. How far are you able to take on inexperienced people and give them training?
6. Do you hire people who are like yourselves?
7. Why do people work in your group?
8. Why do they leave?
9. What would you tell an applicant were the best and worst things about working in your group?
10. Is your group biased towards a particular class? Age range? Sex?
11. Do you have a policy of recruiting local people? Ethnic minorities? Elderly people? School leavers?
12. Do you have a probation period for new staff?
13. How do you get rid of a complete duffer? Please describe one occasion when the group sacked someone/asked them to leave.
14. What happens if someone is undemocratic, or refuses to share?

Quotations

This is the sort of dream job you think you'll run away to London to find.

When the time came for me to leave, they replaced me with a clone - a little me.

People come to us because it's exciting and challenging. The Department says that every malcontent in the field tries us. I think the fact that it isn't a hierarchy is quite attractive. One worker said: 'You know, there are very few places you can tell your boss to fuck off.

You smiled when you thought I was saying the right things and looked at each other when I wasn't. And about half-way through you got quite keen on me and started sitting forward.

Sometimes you can predict that the next recruit will be a woman between 32 and 38.

We do squeeze people out. Criticism is said in forty five different ways to a person's face.

We had a whole layer of assumptions about the people we want to work with - what they should be like. One woman could probably do the job very efficiently; extremely capable. But she's not a feminist, and she's dicey on Unions.

I left but I didn't go away. But I spent a lot of time. People would say: 'What are you doing?' I was doing bits and pieces, but most of what I was doing was re-aligning. I belonged to me again. I could spend days in the park just with me. It became a fascinating thing. Because for two-and a-half years 'me' was something that I practically didn't have time for.

There was a feeling that if we did a team heavy on her she would crack up or something. That she wasn't so resilient to handle that sort of criticism when her own life was in a turmoil. So we held back until it was too late. I don't think we've done her a favour at all. We certainly haven't done ourselves a favour.

Job Rotation and Specialisation

Questions

1. Do you rotate jobs? Why? Please give details.
2. Do you have division of labour or specialisms? Is this a problem?
3. In particular, are there separate administrative workers?
4. Who cleans and defrosts the fridge/scrubs the toilet/rinses the tea towels?
5. How do you extend people's skills and teach new skills? Do you accept someone wanting to stick with the same work?
6. Can you match people's like and dislikes with the functions of the agency? Or can you change your work to let people do what they like?
7. What do you think of expertise?
8. Do people find a conflict between the group's needs and individual needs? What do you do about differences in workers' skills and experiences?

Quotations

When you are at school or college, working together is called cheating.

There is no point in having a collective unless there is collective responsibility - an awareness that you are responsible, not the collective. The collective doesn't take if off you; it puts it on you. It's terribly easy to think: 'Well, the collective will do it'. Which lets you off the hook. And people don't even notice it. It's like the person in the collective household who doesn't see the dirt.

It was the last straw when toilet cleaning got attached to switchboard duty - which I was doing most of the time. And when I brought this up, they said I wasn't a collective type of person.

As you get better you should be able to take on the harder, more complex stuff. What's the point of all those managers developing skills for five or six years and then going for promotion and never using them?

I scrub the toilet. I always scrub the toilet!

We think it's important that someone who saw A in the Advice Centre on Tuesday should see him cleaning the floor in the bookshop on Friday.

Although people have qualifications and experience before they come to us, many of them say that they feel 'deskilled' by joining the unit. The unit operation is itself a training process for all of us.

Admin and finance felt by the collective to be shit-work, dirty work (finance in particular). Lack of interest in it. Administrator especially seen as service worker.

How often does the tail wag the dog? People may get taken on who cannot do the basic job of the Centre. So all sorts of 'project work' is taken on to keep them busy.

Quality Control, Rules and Boundaries

Questions

1. How do you measure or assess the work of people in your group?
2. What do you do if someone isn't pulling their weight?
3. Do people within your group take enthusiasm and commitment for granted?
4. Do you acknowledge an individual working particularly well?
5. Do you evaluate the work of the group as a whole? How?
6. Are there enough criticisms and praises?
7. Do you have rules? In what form? What are they about?
8. How far are your 'rules' an unwritten consensus?
9. Do you use rules as a conservative force? As a means of keeping to the organisation's principles? Because the founders engraved them on tablets of stone?

Quotations

We tend to say there are no rules. Then when a new person does something wrong we say: 'Hey, that's out of play!'.

What we have is a group of colleagues who are peers who can talk to each other who'll help you, but also cut across, criticise and stop you.

They just don't push you to do your best. The team supports you in being mediocre. Maybe creative and individual initiative doesn't fit. And it's very puritan in a way. I mean, it was all right if I was working a lot of hours and got exhausted. That was okay, even if I knew I just wasn't being efficient. I wasted everybody's time chatting. The team should have been critical. They were sympathetic instead.

Generally we have impossibly high expectations of ourselves and our team, and are very critical of each other. You are constantly being put up - not against a set standard - but against how well other people are doing, or how you perceive that. Then, in a funny way, we counter this unreasonable unspoken expectation by being very understanding and accepting of actual performance.

There are some things we don't face up to. Maybe there are, say, three meetings with the same item at the bottom of the agenda - which we don't get to.

I realise it's not neat. There's something in all of us wants it neat. Something in me thinks: 'What we need is a warden'. But life with us is not neat. I wish it was, but it's not. If I got a list of neat rules I would probably be one of the chief messer-uppers.

The fact that we work long hours, or take all sorts of decisions about financial things and management-type things, the Trade Union position would say: 'They are not the sort of decisions that you should be making'.

There's a lot of trust. And he just bullshit us, to tell you the truth. We didn't know he wasn't doing his job properly until he went on holiday and the bills started coming in.

Footnotes

1. This method is discussed in Allen, Thomas H. (1978) *New Methods in Social Science Research*. New York: Praeger.
2. Stanton, Alan (1983) *Collective Working in the Personal Social Services*. Cranfield Institute of Technology, Department of Social Policy.
3. Other thematic headings not included here were Ideology and Politics, The Personal, Outside, Users and Accountability, and Women and Men.

See Alan Stanton (1988) *Windows on Collective Working*. Department of Social Policy, Cranfield Institute of Technology; Alan Stanton (1989) *Invitation to Self-Management*. DabHand Press

The Tutorial System in Social Work Education: Critical Observations and Recommendations

DAVID BAMFORD

Some students get an enormous amount of help and support from their tutors and valued the system highly. Other social work students, on the same course, enjoy radically different tutorial experiences ranging from indifferent to bad, to virtually non-existent. This is blatantly unfair and a recipe for student alienation. With this dual reality emerging from the evidence, the author has tried to build on the positive aspects of social work tutoring and to eradicate the more negative aspects by proposing good practice pointers and guidelines for the future. This is practitioner research directly concerned with 'good practice'. Rather than comparing and contrasting the range of practice, Bamford tries to build upon and develop good practice. In effect, he learns from the mistakes of poor tuition but leans decisively towards the best possible tuition.

This research drew on the words of student social workers, social work tutors, and practice teachers. In doing so it revealed conflicting ideas and vastly different experiences, and positive proposals for the future. David Bamford systematically provides evidence, frameworks for fuller understanding, and a nine point checklist of key areas of concern. When reading this piece it can seem as if some social work tutors felt they were expected to be superhuman in terms of the knowledge and skills required. What's really needed, is a supportive organisational framework, fuller accountability, and clearer agreement about the tasks to be performed (and not to be performed) by a social work tutor. The type of collaborative research worked out with the various groups, and the impressive commitment of the latter all add up to what, for social work, is a relatively unusual empirical effort producing very challenging and disturbing perceptions of the tutorial system in social work education. If those in positions of authority take full note of the calls here for greater accountability, improved quality control systems, and greater clarity of the tutor's role, then it is to be hoped that future social work course students will be encouraged and fulfilled, and of course, social work enhanced - **Editors.**

In this piece I want to examine the implications arising from my fieldwork and, especially the data from many social work students. Altogether the research evidence was gathered from interviews with social work tutors and students concerned with Certificate of Qualification in Social Work (CQSW) in four United Kingdom courses.

My task in this article is to consider the implications of my research findings, and develop a framework for the social work tutor to use in the future. In the light of the evidence I now propose to focus on key issues arising from the research namely: Social work tutoring's organisational structure, tutoring skills and competency levels, the autonomous role of the tutor, and the tutor's relationship work.

Social Work Tutoring's Organisational Structure

Considerations should begin at a very basic level because my own research findings correlated precisely with the earlier findings of Rushton (1976) and Syson (1981), namely individual students on the same social work courses receive tutorial help of immensely variable length and frequency, quite apart from the much more complicated matter of content. Some students received regular tutorials at set times and of a set length. Other students on the same course saw their tutor only very occasionally. The evidence also reveals many and diverse reasons for this state of affairs, ranging from lack of interest on the part of a tutor to a determination on the part of a student to use the tutorial system as little as possible. My first suggestion is therefore that a course regulation should operate which states that each student embarking on a particular CQSW course should have the right of individual access to a personal tutor and should also experience uniformity with colleagues on the course in terms of length and frequency of tutorials. In this way, the infrastructure for an effective and fair system should be created. The evidence revealed an alarming amount of frustration and resentment among students who felt that they did not have sufficient access to their tutors. Some evidence was also forthcoming of tutors finding certain students very elusive. The point about crystallising such an infrastructure is that it would compel the participation of both parties in a way which was unique to the one to one situation. The system would then have the potential to fail not on the grounds of inadequate access but because of the human relations skills or lack of them, of the participants.

Having set up an equitable framework, the next stage is to consider aspects of the tutorial system which emerge from all the available evidence, which seems to be central to an effective and satisfactory tutorial experience, and contribute to an enhanced understanding of the nature of tutoring.

Boundaries Between Tutoring and Lecturing

It is appropriate and prudent to reflect on the type of situations where the personal tutor acts and behaves as a tutor rather than a lecturer. For the most part the research evidence indicated certain types of encounter between these parties that is, individual tutorials, group tutorials, occasionally seminars and other small groups, tripartite meetings, and informal/social settings. Co-researchers did not equate the role of the tutor with the formal lecture situation where the tutor to all intents and purposes, has to become a theorist, and an academic and imparting knowledge giving research evidence etc.

In tutorial situations many students, with the possible exception of those on undergraduate CQSW courses, seem to respond to qualities and aptitudes in the tutor which reflect his/her skill in human relations and their credibility and right to be a social work tutor rather than 'merely' a tutor. A lot of students look to the tutorial as the forum where any concept can be discussed, but where the individual, personalised developmental issues, of which there were many examples in my research can be addressed.

In the tripartite situation, practice teachers expected tutors to be relatively in touch with contemporary practice and at least able to understand the relevance and importance of the skills being taught. In the research the tutor who peddled techniques and methods without ever having tested them in practice was an object of particular derision. A significant part of the evidence from practice teachers revealed tutors who were uncomfortable in social work agencies and who sometimes retreated to the safety of (an) abstract theoretical interpretations. Often they then felt undervalued in this role.

The College Environment and the Tutor: The Inherent Bias Towards Theory?

My research revealed that many tutors felt alienated and undervalued in Higher Education settings, even within departments which on the face of it have a considerable professional/vocational emphasis.

Their desire to be empathic and responsive to students, to retain practice credibility so that they don't become deskilled and fossilised and have up to date teaching and case material (was) afforded no recognition whatsoever within college. All of the kudos and rewards in terms of status and promotion depended upon them drifting away from student centred work and towards research and publications. Thus several tutors felt themselves to be in a classic double bind situation. On the one hand, credibility with heads of department and non social work academic colleagues depended on traditional academic activities. On the other hand credibility with students and the external worlds of social work including practice teachers depended to a great extent on staying in touch with practice and being a credible figure first and foremost as a social worker. Current students found it impossible to respect a social work tutor who had drifted away completely from the realities of the coalface and had become either an academic researcher or a course administrator. For practice teachers the issue was that they wanted a tutor who understood and was comfortable with social work practice concepts.

Some tutors seemed quite happy with conventional academic life and regarded students, the tutorial system, and tripartites, as an irritant time wasting distraction. Tutors were largely unaware of the resentment and alienation felt by students and practice teachers, because of their inaccessibility and because of their disinterest in focusing on those person-centred developmental issues so often the priority of students. In essence, the issue here is one of how higher education is conceived and understood. I believe that the tutor who is interested in professional practice and has high credibility with students should be valued as highly as the tutor who devotes much more energy to research interests and publications and who may, for example, have a much smaller number of tutees. Both types should be not merely tolerated or even accommodated, but actually valued equally by their department and faculty. In this way tutors with different strengths and aptitudes could freely choose their own directions without at the same time sacrificing their chances of increased status and promotion. Suffice it to say that the 'tyrannical academic ideology' which was devastated by Bramley (1977) and others is, in the light of my research, alive, well and living in social work departments in Ireland, (although it is also true that a few tutors were trying very hard to combine practice interests and research in their external activities).

The next aspect of college environment and the tutor I wish to consider is the relationship between social work tutors and other academic staff. Two of the four groups of tutors felt themselves to be under attack from their non social work academic colleagues. This pressure tended sometimes to be covert, insidious, and associated with a certain contempt for the notion of professional as opposed to purely academic education. The rigour of academic standards on social work courses was regarded as highly suspect, and the objectives of social work education which are much broader than the solely intellectual training of most academic courses were both rejected and simply not understood. The result of this tension was that tutors running CQSW courses felt themselves under real pressure to equate intellectual excellence with social work practice competence and therefore demand the highest cognitive standards of their students at the expense of other developmental objectives at least as important. Interestingly, there was also evidence that tutors have succumbed to this pressure. At other times the pressure from academic colleagues was not merely snide and covert, but actually overt, with calls at faculty meetings to shut down social work courses because they lowered the academic tone of the university.

On the other hand there were also examples of individual tutors, and indeed one staff group in particular who not only could 'hold their own' with colleagues on academic grounds but also revelled in conventional academic life. The fascinating factor here is that these were also the tutors with the least time for a tutorial system and, in the eyes of students, least equipped.

Tutoring Skills and Competency Levels

I now propose to isolate and analyse, in the light of the evidence, the essential aptitudes and qualities which the personal tutor in social work education should have according to social work and students views. Essentially students valued humanistic more than to an academic approach, and individual rather than group tutorials were the norm.

The evidence suggested that given a high level of sensitivity on the part of the tutor, the student, through the tutorial experience, can engage much more fully with a course and use the tutor to work through a series of important personal developmental issues. A significant number of tutors recognised this and were acutely aware that students tended to use them as role models for social work practice. Students wanted a tutor with sufficient sensitivity, awareness and ability to pick up on the more personalised developmental issues provoked by the course.

Regrettably, very strong evidence was forthcoming which suggested that many tutors did not operate in this personal way. Some were disinterested and regarded students as a distraction from their research, some stuck to the academic consultant type of tutoring, (a model which took an unholy battering from students) some were so preoccupied by the organisation of placements and other duties that students as individuals were invisible, and finally some were perceived as being incapable by students.

The Tutor's Relationship with Social Work Practice: The Need to Avoid Obfuscation and Fossilisation

One may well ask the question why so many tutors are deficient in relationships when, theoretically at least, all have a significant practical background?

First of all and most starkly, some evidence emerged which indicated that a minority of social work tutors had in fact extremely limited or indeed no social work practice experience. 'Fossilisation' as a category has four dimensions; the tutor with no practice experience at all; the tutor with no recent practice experience; the tutor who attempted to teach often quite trendy and novel methods of social work intervention, but who had no experiential basis for teaching them; and last the tutor who over the years had become remote and totally regarded himself as a course administrator. Students and practice teachers expected tutors to be in touch and relatively up to date with practice in an experiential sense. They identified a strong correlation between this and credibility, authenticity, and an ability to empathise with the course experience as felt by students. The strength of this research evidence, coincides with views expressed by Ho (1975), Tropp (1970), and Harper (1984), namely that the tutors should have a substantial practice background, and also a commitment to stay up to date with practice experientially.

The Problem of Achieving Authentic Communication in Tutorials

It is difficult not to be struck by the extent of the research evidence which centred on unsatisfactory communication in tutorials. The key issue is to do with the tutor creating a climate which helps the student shift from a position which is purely self-protective to a position where she feels sufficiently safe and secure to choose her own social work directions. The research evidence strongly suggests that then and only then will an authentic and congruent dialogue be achieved. Otherwise students employ a spectrum of survival strategies which can range from deliberately using a personal tutor as little as possible to a kind of instrumental acquiescence, pretending to internalise the perspectives held dear by one's personal tutor. The evidence confirms the views of Heraud (1981) and Levy (1976) that students simply will not risk a frank levelling debate with their tutor if the latter has not got the flexibility and capacity to accommodate this without threatening the student's status as a passing student. In several categories we saw evidence of students playing the system's game (as Richan and Mendelsohn (1973) have observed) namely that social work students expose just enough of themselves to get through the course but not enough to be personally bruised in the process.

The alarming thing about this evidence was the extent to which tutors were 'taken in' by these highly convincing student survival strategies. If tutors were genuine, flexible, democratic, and person centred then the student tended to gradually relax and get a lot out of the system including a freedom to disagree and challenge. But if the messages were hierarchical, status conscious, and belittling, the student quickly worked out a strategy to survive.

The Autonomous Role of the Tutor

Without doubt from the viewpoint of students the research evidence suggests that this was the area which aroused the greatest confusion and suspicion. On the one hand students related many examples of not understanding the potential role of the tutor and what agendas could be pursued. On the other hand many students were deeply suspicious about the content of the tutorials and the motives of the tutor, fearing some sort of hidden and covert assessment of them as potential social workers which involved some sort of intellectual, psychological and attitudinal striptease. The most infuriating thing about this 'hidden curriculum' from the student's viewpoint was their difficulty in prising it out into the open. They found that several tutors would deny the existence of such a comprehensive assessment even if students were utterly convinced it was happening. Many examples illustrated the various ways in which students discovered their tutor's profile on them, such as in tripartite meetings or in a report lying on a desk and this provided the justification of student anger and resentment. The whole point about bringing this assessment process out into the open would be to make it more valid because students would have the opportunity to agree or disagree at any point on the course. In many ways students regarded this covert assessment as much more important compared to the obvious, tangible, assessed elements on the course such as assignments, projects, and examinations, simply because they felt its impact a lot more. The four groups of tutors involved in the research did for the most part concur, after much heartsearching, that this was a real and much bigger issue than they imagined. For practice teacher's the hidden curriculum was a constant reality because frequently at tripartite meetings the full extent of the tutors' profile on the student would be unpacked and used to influence the practice teachers assessment of the student.

The Problem of Differing Approaches, Ideologies and Priorities of Individual Tutors

There are probably two main things which could be done to help the many students who felt trapped by the priorities and pet theories of their tutor. Firstly, there is a need to define a common base line agenda for tutorials which will be addressed by all tutors regardless of their individual perspectives. If this was achieved, then tutors on the same course could at least attempt to achieve uniformity. Presumably it would have to be linked to the three sets of general course objectives, academic, instrumental, and expressive referred to above.

The second thing which could be done is to introduce an element of choice of tutor at the start of training. There was no evidence at all this was ever considered on any of the courses researched. Students were simply allocated a tutor and had absolutely no say in the matter. Yet choice seems such a logical concept to introduce because tutors have very different areas of specialist knowledge and expertise, just as many students will have particular concepts and contexts of practice which they might wish to explore. If a detailed profile on the background and major interests of each tutor was made available to a new group of students, they could be offered a choice of tutor subject to practical matters. These two steps might go some way to accommodating the fact and legitimacy of a spectrum of positions within social work education and practice. Without claiming that this is the correct or only answer I would expect that they would also create the 'right' climate of co-operative partnership between tutors and students right from the start of training.

Tutors and Practice Teachers

What many practice teachers want from tutors is a well thought out, integrated, supportive function but several tutors were perceived as distant from the coalface, disinterested in tripartite work, and imbued with academic snobbery and arrogance. Theoretical interpretations of practice are often what tutors expect from students, and the examination of techniques, methods and skills of social work practice which is mainly what practice teachers expect of students. Some may say that the tensions arising from these differing needs is inevitable or even desirable, but it does leave students in an exceptionally awkward position as both parties 'complete for their mind'. Third, the evidence revealed how difficult many tutors find it to relinquish their primary dyadic role with a student for the duration of a placement and allow the practice teacher autonomy in assessment. It is much better I propose, to openly acknowledge that the tutor has a role in relation to student assessment, this can enhance the overall assessment. Fourth, tutors and courses are heavily dependent upon the goodwill of practice teachers and agencies and for this reason they have an absurdly high level of tolerance for perceived incompetency. Most choose the pragmatic path of tiptoe diplomacy to avoid ruffling feathers and antagonising people who regarded as 'resources' may be irreplaceable. I got no sense of a similar double bind among practice teachers, although they did on occasions show some insight into the dilemmas faced by tutors.

Students' concerns' about the hidden curriculum help to spotlight an important issue, that is the importance of clarifying and focusing on the role of the tutor at the start of professional training. I now propose to go through a list of nine key points which emerged from the research evidence and which might go some way to clearing up the confusion and suspicion which abounds about the roles of the social work tutor.

Nine Practice Pointers for Tutors
The tutor as a provider
It is the tutor's responsibility to get to know the student as an individual and work out the best course experiences to ensure maximum personal development. So much is implicit in this role, for example an ability to establish a rapport with the student, to be credible in the eyes of the student, to be accessible and approachable, to combine support and challenge, and to encourage in the student a capacity for critical self-evaluation.

The tutor as an accountable assessor
At present, tutors have far too much freedom to use their opinions of students in an unstructured way and without being called to account for them. Tutors need to acknowledge more openly that they are constantly formulating impressions, which become opinions which in turn lead to firmly held beliefs concerning the needs and abilities of the students. They also need to acknowledge that these views are used to influence the course experience of students, to nudge them in certain directions, to look for a

particular type of practice teacher, to focus a project differently and to become more aware of this impact on other groups.

The clearest evidence of this hidden curriculum came from the tutors' groups. They provided examples of tutors fiercely defending their qualitative opinions of student abilities in examination board meetings when the evidence for those opinions could not be linked with performance on the actual assessed elements of the course. I would certainly advocate that personal tutors should provide a written tutor profile on each student to be discussed with each student and to be submitted to an examination board. Such a system could easily borrow from the enlightened ideas on the 'profile system' emanating from secondary education. For example, Fletcher (1980) analysed the very detailed profile system at Sutton Centre Community School and commented on it as being 'far-thinking, democratic and egalitarian', with the ultimate goal being 'non-alienative education'. The evidence confirms that often the opinions of tutors regarding students are not only qualitative and impressionistic but also partially or totally in error. The profiling system would go some way to limiting the discretionary power of tutors and make their personalised comments legitimate statements, open for discussion.

One tutor commented that just as he would not expect his student to be anything other than consultative and democratic in his social work with clients, so he could not in conscience depart from the same approach as a tutor.

The tutor as a 'sweeper'
This area is, possibly, the least contentious. Most tutors had little difficulty associating their role with helping the individual student make theoretical and conceptual links between the various elements of a professional social work course. It was immensely reassuring to have the personal tutor acting as a fulcrum for the entire course experience, explaining, clarifying, redirecting and illustrating the inter-relevance, of concepts with skill and panache. To adequately fulfil this particular function, the tutor clearly requires not only human relations skills, but also a specialised knowledge of social work theory, and a sound all round knowledge of the key academic disciplines associated with social work.

The tutor as a sound administrator
The evidence suggests that this was one of the least popular but most time consuming parts of the job from the viewpoint of

tutors. Virtually all commented on the incredible amount of time taken up on placement business with and on behalf of individual students. There seemed to be no easy way round the delicate negotiation with agencies, and the consultations with students which were primarily concerned with mere practicalities. Many yearned for the days, as was the case when they did their course, when a list would be posted and no dialogue at all would take place with students.

The tutor as a confidant

A significant amount of evidence emerged which revealed the personal tutor in the role of supporting the student through a problematic personal situation which, in part at least, had been provoked by some aspect of the total course experience. A number of students expressed genuine gratitude in referring to very personal, confidential and intricate life situations with which their tutors had worked. Some tutors expressed the view that professional training in social work can frequently destabilise a student's personal life and because of this they had an ethical duty to respond, and in doing so operationalise some of their own social work skills. For the most part they also recognised the dangers inherent in the temptation to play the social worker at every available opportunity. One obvious dilemma was not having sufficient space to deal adequately with a particular situation. Another problem for the tutor was to decide at what point a student should be referred on to the college counsellors, and how to handle this transfer without damaging or alienating the student. All tutors, whether they were prepared to act as a confidant or not, were fully aware of the controversy surrounding this confidant role. There was a general acceptance that tutors, particularly those with a strong social work practice identification, could easily drift into this role, something that some students would be quick to exploit.

The other aspect of this role also depends on the awareness and sensitivity of the tutor to detect and deal with the anxieties and feelings of insecurity which the student might have. Much of the evidence from students and tutors illustrates how deeply many students can be shaken by the impact of professional social work training. The evidence showed some tutors with the capacity to pick up and deal with the affective impact of training, often instilled a new sense of confidence and self-belief in the student.

The tutor as a constructive critic

This role could be characterised as the sharp edge of tutoring where the tutor might challenge the student and on occasions directly confront. Implicit in this is a capacity to cope with conflict, and be sufficiently robust to work through phases of tension and disagreement. In doing this and in not avoiding potentially conflictual issues with the student, the tutor will undoubtedly provoke antagonism and resentment on a temporary basis. Yet the evidence from former students in particular is very much in favour of the 'strong firm hand' and the capacity to 'lay it on the line' when necessary.

The tutor as studies adviser

As with the 'sweeper' function, this tutoring task emerged as primarily an academic exercise to do with advising and helping students in relation to assignment work, project work, reading material, etc. All tutors accepted this function as a dimension of tutoring. Some, however, saw it as the beginning and end of their overall role as a tutor. Most students were heavily critical of this limited interpretation which left untouched so much of the overall impact of professional training. However, I suspect, that for the tutor with a limited background in social work or for the tutor who is becoming preoccupied with traditional academic culture a rigid adherence to this academic adviser interpretation of the role may be a necessary though unhelpful survival mechanism.

The tutor as catalyst

Essentially, this role emerged from the research evidence through situations where the tutor stimulated the potential of the student and activated resources which the student might not have been fully aware of possessing. The tutor as catalyst was demonstrated when tutors revealed sufficient maturity to release students to discover their own perspectives and potentials. It was not possible to act as a catalyst if one also expected students to become theoretical and practical replicas of oneself. The tutors who is successfully assumed the role of a catalyst gave student-centred work their top priority, with enthusiasm, commitment, and, often, charisma.

The tutor as student negotiator / advocate

This particular role had four main dimensions all of which highlighted work on behalf of, rather than directly with, students: securing particular practice placements; clarifying students skills when not fully acknowledged to practice teachers; clarifying students knowledge and skills, when necessary in examination board meetings, and finally, providing references for prospective employers.

Practice placements much depended on the subtlety, diplomacy, and general human relations skill of the tutor attempting to redirect, comment and interpret, without alienating and antagonising either one of the other two parties involved.

The Adoption of Children
with Learning Difficulties

CATHERINE MACASKILL

*One of the most fundamental and increasingly important functions of practitioner research in social work is its educative role. In this striking piece the educative function goes beyond providing new knowledge to detailing practical as well as policy implications in the area of adoption of children with learning difficulties. These implications cover the main areas of recruitment, assessment of, and support for adoptive families. They are drawn from original data obtained from adoptive parents and siblings, as well as social workers in voluntary organisations. The research points to the tensions that exist within professionals distanced from adoption cases involving children with learning difficulties and the adoptive families themselves. Informed practical suggestions are made to aid all relevant parties so that the transitions involved in these adoptions are more sensitive and smooth. The enthusiasm of the researcher for the families and the siblings, is tempered into a good practice checklist. An imaginative child 'interviewing' technique, was a crucial feature in its success. The evidence is embedded in each recommendation. So, too, there is a thoroughly professional solidarity with the adoptive families - **Editors**.*

Background to the Research Topic

Changes in British adoption practice have been affected by American influence and up until quite recently only healthy babies were originally considered to be eligible for adoption. Any child who failed to pass a rigorous and thorough medical examination was excluded from the adoption process. A recent upsurge of new thinking has altered this situation. During the 1970s the principle that no child is unadoptable regardless of his or her degree of difficulty began to be translated into British adoption practice from America. There, new groups of children who began to find new families became known as the 'hard to place'. They included children of school age, teenagers, children with learning difficulties, children from a variety of racial groups and groups of siblings of varying ages. Britain began to identify similar groups of children within its culture who had previously been labelled 'unadoptable', and so a new era in British adoption practice dawned.

The research presented here coincides with a critical stage in the development of new concepts and new models of practice within the field of adoption. The availability of the status of adoption for children with learning difficulties is perhaps the most radical of all changes within adoption.

Serious misconceptions and an aura of mystery have always surrounded people with learning difficulties. A history of concealing and confining people with learning difficulties in custodial wards in closed institutions has done little to diminish public prejudice.

The most stereotyped group among people with learning difficulties are Downs Syndrome. Beginning with the unfortunate term 'mongoloid' and reinforced by the emphasis on physical features, the traditional approach to mongolism was to characterise these people as a 'race apart', or as unfinished children. Today we have changed names. We do not now categorise people with learning difficulties as imbeciles or idiots, but are our perceptions any different? In recent years, an unprecedented attack has been made on the public conscience through official documentation.[1] All advocate the principle of community care for children with learning difficulties, yet 'results' have been slow to emerge. Adoption is one form of community care for children with learning difficulties.

Research Design
Finding the adoptive families
The first main task involved in designing this research study was to find a group of adoptive families of children with learning difficulties. Two main routes towards adoptive families seemed possible, through the statutory sector or through the voluntary sector. I chose the latter route, through adoption societies, because of the innovatory nature of the adoption of children with learning difficulties. Therefore it seemed logical to expect to find a larger number of more complex placements happening through this source. I decided to draw on a sample of children with learning difficulties taken from six adoption societies, which included 20 families at different stages in the process of adopting a child with learning difficulties. These adoption societies form an interesting group. Three were newly set up to promote the adoption of 'hard to place' children, and are pioneers in this work. The other three were originally baby placing agencies, but have gradually transferred to this 'new' type of adoption. The latter group have regularly experienced struggles as they have attempted to break away from traditional concepts and ideas. Those which were

'purpose-built' have been able to select new staff, and begin with a fresh approach and outlook.

I began from the premise that I wanted to include children who had obvious and significant learning difficulties, and that the greater the degree of learning difficulty, the more relevant the placement was for inclusion in the research. The majority of the 23 children who were eventually selected for (the study) research fell within the severe learning difficulties range, and fitted broadly within the following criteria:

1. Children whose physical appearance immediately conveyed the impression of having a learning difficulty.
2. Children who were often categorised by professionals under certain common headings (for example Down's Syndrome, Cerebral Palsy).
3. Children with major problems in learning who required help through special education.
4. Children who would be unlikely to achieve a fully independent life-style throughout adolescence and adulthood.

I felt that children who met those criteria would be most likely to throw into focus the difficulties which adoptive parents face in caring for a child with learning difficulties. The total group of 23 children with learning difficulties consisted of 13 pre-school children and ten school age children.

Regarding stages of placement during the research only one 12 year old boy with learning difficulties had not been permanently placed with his new family. Delays occurred because of the difficulty in securing a school place for him in the adoptive family's local area. All the other children with learning difficulties had been in placement for varying lengths of time, from four months to four and half years. Information about their medical and social history was obtained from adoption agencies. Valuable data was also obtained from interviews with adoptive parents, with siblings living within the adoptive families studied, and with various professional and semi-professional staff involved. These included adoption society social workers and the Directors or project leaders of each of the six adoption societies involved in placing the 23 children with learning difficulties, the subject of the research. In general terms there interviews were structured and semi structured and recorded the views and experiences of those mainly involved in a process which led to each of the 23 children being formally adopted. Of special note, I think, was the way the questionnaire format was adapted for siblings in adoptive families.

To begin with it was called a 'family funsheet' and not a questionnaire. Instead of a 'dry' list of typed out questions on plain A4 paper it was decided to make the questionnaire more child friendly. It was especially designed for 9-12 year olds, and was done by drawing a sort of picture frame around each page using a variety of small friendly symbols and shapes. These included flowers and leaves, teddy bears, faces and building bricks. The latter was, for example, set against the question 'draw your favourite toys'. Also both happy and sad children's faces were set in the spaces against the questions `What makes (adopted child's name) cry?'. `What does (name) do that makes you happy?'. The willingness and enthusiasm of the children to take part in this research seemed to be closely associated with four factors; the encouragement and interest from parents, the emphasis by me that the research activities would be good fun, my approach of getting alongside the children as they completed their fun sheets, and a worksheet which combined a variety of different activities to retain the children's interest. Overall the patterned and picture framed affect was to provide a friendly and useful research instrument and good fun for respondents.[2] In one question and of 31 terms (such as nice, noisy, sad, happy) offered to younger respondents to describe their adopted sibling the term `learning difficulty' was never used. In other words the `new' family members were seen as just that, with their own personality, and not ascribed the `learning difficulty' label. As I will describe later, such labelling when it did take place, was reserved for those at a more physical and emotional distance from the adoption experience.

Conclusions arising from the research

The adoption of children with learning difficulties is still at an innovatory stage in Britain. It is commonly believed that the slow development of this work is due to lack of public interest in adopting children with learning difficulties. This theory is questionable. It is impossible to read about the experiences of the families who took part in this research without being impressed by their willingness and eagerness to take a child with learning difficulties into their family. The surprising finding is that their interest and enthusiasm was often obstructed rather than encouraged by professional attitudes and approaches. The conclusion of this study is therefore that professional attitudes towards children with learning difficulties, and towards the type of families who volunteer for this task, are major barriers to the progress of work. One noticeable exception to this was the practice of adoption society social workers, but even they sometimes allowed a personal view of learning difficulties to influence their work.

It was striking to note the contrasting perceptions of professionals and adoptive families. Professionals labelled the child with learning difficulties as different from normal children and tended to set them apart from others by emphasising their weaknesses, difficulties and abnormalities. In contrast, adoptive families responded to the individual personalities of children with learning difficulties and began from the standpoint of recognising the child's potential strengths. It was not just that professionals were influenced by preconceived ideas about learning difficulties, they also did not recognise that families were using a very different conceptual framework to understand it.

The real stories of adoptive families indicate that professional assumptions about the detrimental effects of adopting a child with learning difficulties were often wrong. Instead of bringing major problems to families, children with learning difficulties brought a new measure of vitality. The enthusiasm and commitment of adoptive parents was usually reflected in the excitement of other children in the family, while the child with learning difficulties made remarkable progress, and often reached milestones which had been thought to be completely beyond their limited capacity. We are therefore brought face to face with total families thriving as a consequence of this type of adoption.

There were encouraging signs throughout this research that negative attitudes can be transformed into positive ones, and this is a hopeful indicator for the future of this work. Changes of attitudes were usually effected when people moved close to the child with learning difficulties and his or her enthusiastic adoptive family. Adoption society social workers, adoption panel members and relatives and friends of adoptive families were forced to relinquish their prejudices by this means. The closer people moved to the real experiences of adoptive families, the more likely they were to be positively influenced while those who remained at a distance retained their original negative approach. This points to the relevance of using experienced adoptive families to educate professionals and other prospective adoptive families.

The multi-disciplinary nature of learning difficulties creates unique problems. A diversity of professional attitudes and approaches creates confusion for families and seriously impedes the work. A coordinated team approach should be an essential ingredient of any service available to families with a child with learning difficulties. Teamwork implies that professionals work together towards a common goal. A firm professional belief in the value of an adoption service for children with learning difficulties is therefore the first step towards achieving a coordinated and effective adoption service. Here I want to concentrate on the 'good practice' implications for adopting children with learning difficulties, as raised by the researchers findings.

Implications for Adoption Practice: Towards a 'Good Practice' Checklist
Recruitment of adoptive families

The use of photographs of specific children is a useful method of attracting public interest in adoption, and may be the first means of informing the public about the existence of a particular adoption project. The account in a popular journal (*Woman's Own; Family Circle*) of a successful adoption depicting unusual features about the adoptive family, and details about the child with learning difficulties, helps to convey the changing nature of adoption practice. People are able to measure the likelihood of their acceptability as adopters against this information. Families who are looking for a challenging type of parenthood find their interest aroused by reading about the child's difficulties. Other people who are unfamiliar with learning difficulties are likely to be frightened by the use of labels, and to be attracted by the child's photograph and information about his or her interests. The content of the written text will depend on the type of audience which adoption societies are aiming to reach. The attraction of the public to a photograph of a child with learning difficulties is rarely associated with a child's good looks. In fact, the opposite is the case. The first impression of some adoptive parents in this study was that their child was rather unattractive. They experienced an unspoken message being conveyed to them from the child's picture which was associated with the child's forlorn state and special need for parents. Certain children should not be excluded from use in publicity because they may appear to social workers to be unappealing.

Preparing adoptive parents and families

Spending time in the homes of natural and adoptive parents of children with learning difficulties, searching for useful resources, visits to small informal groups for children with learning difficulties, voluntary work at a pre-school playgroup, and undertaking a direct caring role for children with learning difficulties in a residential unit, were all examples of practical preparation which families found helpful.

In the research the value of individual interviews with social workers was mainly associated with the creation of personal links between adopters and their social workers. Families derived minimal knowledge from these interviews. The possibility of reducing the amount of time which social workers spend in interviews with families should be seriously considered.

By contrast group preparation was a very useful source of learning. Contact with other experienced adoptive families at these meetings enabled some people to consider adopting a child with learning difficulties for the first time. The idea of including the child with learning difficulties with parents at group meetings was an excellent way of breaking down public prejudice to children with learning difficulties.

Preparing siblings and sharing information

The availability of advice from social workers about how to prepare other children in the family would prevent parents from struggling with this task on a trial and error basis. The term 'learning difficulty' or, especially, the term 'mental handicap', used in the past is likely to have negative connotations for children who have never had close contact with a child with learning difficulties. Contact with real children with learning difficulties helps to dispel these fantasies. It may not always be possible to create informal links with other siblings of adopted children with learning difficulties, but this opportunity should not be bypassed when it is practically feasible.

In the research the information which was shared with families about children with learning difficulties tended to over-emphasis the child's disabilities, and omit details about potential. It would be helpful if a more balanced picture of the child could be presented, incorporating positive as well as negative features.

Written information is useful for adopters. Adopters valued the opportunity to have direct access to the child's case file. Even those people who had considerable difficulty understanding some of the terms used in reports, interpreted this gesture as a clear indication of the confidence which the adoption society had in them.

Preparation of residential staff and foster parents for their role in the placements

It is not only adoptive families who require preparation for adoption, the child's previous carers also need help if they are to make a maximum contribution towards the success of the placement. Difficulties were most likely to occur when responsibility for organising introductory visits was left entirely between adopters and previous carers, without social work intervention. Complex emotions are liable to arise at this stage in the adoption process, and therefore the active involvement of social workers with previous carers and adopters is crucial. Wherever possible, introductions should not be commenced before a school place, where appropriate, has been secured.

Protracted introductory meetings are especially stressful for adoptive families and the child with learning difficulties and they should be planned, purposeful and properly co-ordinated.

Support During the Post-Placement Period
The social workers' role during the post-placement period

The social workers' role during the post-placement period will vary according to each family situation. Some families will want to retain close contact with their social worker, while others will prefer to function in an independent manner. The social worker's personal warmth and encouragement were features which adopters appreciated during this period.

Ensuring that families are linked with appropriate local resources is an important aspect of the social workers' role. There was some evidence to suggest that when these links are instigated and strengthened during the pre-placement period, they are more likely to be effectively utilised by adopters after the arrival of their child with learning difficulties.

Adoptive families did not consider that their social worker was the most appropriate person to help them through practical problems with their child. They attributed this expertise to people who already had some direct experience of working with children.

The extended family as a support system

The support of the extended family enhanced the quality of the placement. The immediate availability of a baby-sitting service, temporary respite care and empathetic listeners, were all contained within the family network and facilitated the smooth running of the placement. This support system is susceptible to change especially as grandparents grow too elderly to be able to help in an active way and it is important for social workers to be alert to the effect of such changes.

Respite care

Any event which causes disruption of the children with learning difficulties regular routines is likely to create difficulties. Even families who cope well under normal circumstances may require practical help for temporary periods at times of crisis. Adopters who do not have family support are particularly vulnerable. Difficulties with school age children with learning difficulties, which are liable to arise during holiday periods can be alleviated by the availability of a holiday playscheme. It would have been helpful if this service had been more readily available in every area.

The aim of integrating children with learning difficulties is not likely to be realised unless time is spent with the leaders of youth groups and voluntary organisations so that careful preparation can be made for their inclusion in normal activities.

The use of support groups
Support groups for parents of children with learning difficulties are mainly composed of natural parents of children with learning difficulties and, therefore, adoptive parents may feel unhappy about attending. The parents in this study who persevered with attendance were not only able to benefit themselves, but also gained personal satisfaction from opportunities to help other natural parents of children with learning difficulties.

The support of experienced adoptive parents
The potential of experienced adoptive families of children with learning difficulties to help new adopters at times of practical difficulty with their child, was not utilised to its full extent. This type of help concurs with adopters' perceptions about wanting to use people with direct experience of children, but it is essential to create stronger links in the pre-placement period if this resource is to be used in a spontaneous manner.

Post adoption support
Some people consider it to be disadvantageous for families to adopt children with learning difficulties because they assume that families will want to sever all contact with professionals as soon as the adoption is finalised. This idea flows from a traditional view of the adoption of babies. The decision to adopt did not prevent families in this study from continuing to use a social work service. The type of post-placement service which was most acceptable to them was one where they felt that their experiences were being used constructively by the adoption society to help other prospective adopters. In this way they were giving assistance to others at the same time as they were receiving help for themselves.

The lifestyles of families who adopt a child with learning difficulties point to the appropriateness of a post adoption service: they lived from day to day, tackling problems as they encountered them and were rarely interested in absorbing knowledge which was not of immediate practical relevance.

Wider Education: A Team Approach

It is important for discussion and debate to begin between social work, education, medical and paramedical groups so that differing attitudes towards adoption of children with learning difficulties can be fully explored. How can we expect public interest in this work to grow if professionals continue to retain lethargic and negative attitudes towards the positive value of adoption of children with learning difficulties? In-service training on this subject is incomplete without the involvement of professional people from a wide variety of disciplines.

Footnotes

1. HMSO, 1971; HMSO, 1979; DHSS, 1976; DHSS, 1977; DHSS, 1977a

2. The remaining questions for this 9-12 age group were: 'Draw or describe your family' 'Does Anyone in the family have a nick-name?' 'Tell me more about (adopted child's name)', 'Can you think of anything that - cannot do?' 'What is - good at?' 'What do you and ...play together?' 'Do you ever quarrel?' 'What makes...happy?' 'What does...do that makes you angry?'. Respondent siblings in the older, 13-16 year age group were not asked these detailed questions but instead asked to 'write an (imaginary) letter' to friends describing what life is like with a sibling who has learning difficulties.

Part Six
Reflections on the Experiences

The Crucial Issue: Obtaining Agreement for Practitioner Research

NICKI CORNWELL

This piece vividly portrays the 'political' problems which can occur when undertaking practitioner research. The problems centre on obtaining permission and negotiating access when the research involves one's employing authority, researcher's worries about 'failing to produce the goods', employer's fears about the research findings, and finally, the effect of undertaking research on the professional's own practice. The tensions that can and do occur when occupying the dual role of social work practitioner and practitioner - researcher are well illustrated.

Nicki Cornwell describes the `politics' involved in studying a new assessment process in special education. There are moments of fear and loathing. There are other moments of quick thinking and skilful movement. Practitioners are invariably acutely aware of their local and domestic politics. When engaged in research they very often use this awareness most astutely. `Practice-wisdom' of the 'how to play the system' variety should never be under-rated. For many, playing the system changes from a necessary nuisance into a revealing study in itself. The method used is that of story telling, an autobiographical account of events, thoughts and decisions. Others may readily `see themselves' in the account. Yet its aim is not to generalise. This is a cautionary tale which is put into content in the subsequent chapter -
Editors.

The assessment process that I studied had been set up as a result of the Education Act 1981. The process acts as a gateway to special education, and is managed by the local education authority. The authority are obliged to consult 'experts' from Education, Health and Social Services, and to seek the views of parents before arriving at a decision about appropriate educational provision for a child who may have special needs. At the end of this process, known as 'Statementing', the authority issues a statement of the educational provision that is to be made for the child. I am going to try to describe the negotiations that eventually succeeded in persuading a mixture of parents and professionals to participate in the research project. At the time I was working as a social worker attached to a special school and responsible (eventually) to the manager of the process that I was investigating - the Assistant Director of Special Services (Education Department).

Selling the Research Idea

Persuading people to take part in research projects can be difficult. A great deal of groundwork has to be carried out to obtain interviews with identified people. This is especially true if you are proposing to carry out a piece of individual research. It is analogous to being an unknown singer persuading the manager of a club to give you a spot on the bill: a prestigious and well-known group making a similar request is more likely to have it granted.

There is an added problem if in addition you are not quite clear about what it is that you intend to study. Thus my first request to the Assistant Director was for leave of absence and travelling expenses to take up a place on an MPhil course to study problems in interprofessional co-operation. I had a sinking feeling that I had tried to sell 'something' to raise interest, without quite knowing 'what' I was selling, I had made promises that something would happen and began to think 'What happens if I can't deliver any goods?'.

As my intentions became clearer, I had the difficult task of negotiating an agreement to carry out a case study of the assessment process for which the Assistant Director was responsible. I wanted to interview the consumers of the service, staff whose participation could be 'required', and others over whom the Assistant Director had no jurisdiction. This second interview with the Assistant Director was crucial. Misgivings had to be recognised and allayed. These centred around the potential political delicacy of research findings in view of existing concerns about communication problems in the newly devised assessment process. I conveyed the information that there could, if necessary, be restricted access to research theses, but I did not think that it would be required. I used the phrase 'polite political evasions', which seemed to have a powerful impact. I reminded the Assistant Director of my interest in issues of interprofessional co-operation and felt I was being pressured to provide assurances about and in advance of the research findings (which, of course, could not be given).

I had collected information about what happens in other authorities which I was able to offer to share. I indicated that I wanted to interview professionals, office staff including the Assistant Director, and parents of children who had been assessed. I agreed to a request that parents should be contacted with a cover letter from the Assistant Director. I agreed to lodge the questionnaire(s) with the Assistant Director 'should queries from councillors arise'. I went away with agreement to support the research.

I began to try to interest targeted groups informally, whilst preparing the questionnaires. I felt like a salesperson, selling future promises. Phrases like 'improving service delivery', and 'identifying gaps in provision' tripped off my tongue. I gathered more understanding of where there were problems in communication, and my knowledge of vested interests began to grow.

The cover letter was not yet ready when I needed it which led to inevitable procrastination in dispatching the questionnaires, but I put this down to lack of interest and other service demands rather than inventional obstructiveness. It was frustrating. I quickly offered to draft one, thus regaining some control over the contents. After two sets of corrections, my draft letter was accepted and the questionnaires lodged as agreed. The questionnaires looked harmless: questions about what worried parents most, what were the professional concerns, the most memorable experience...many people do not realise just what a lethal tool simple questions can be, when asked sympathetically and systematically.

Research as a Bargaining Process: The Personal Approach

I decided to ask a Health Centre to act as a postbox, hoping but not certain that this could 'neutralise' the effect of the cover letter from the Education Office. Parents were sent a stamped addressed envelope, and a form to return in which they were asked if they were willing or unwilling to be interviewed. A sub sample of three Asian families were approached personally by an Asian colleague who agreed to act as interpreter.

Seventeen out of 20 families from the first sample were interviewed. What did this indicate, given the apathetic response reported by the Department?

Negotiating Interviews and Establishing Trust

Whilst working out how to contact parents, I had been negotiating the goodwill of the educational psychologists. I knew that there would be difficulties because of the fraught communication between the Assistant Director and the service. They could not really refuse if required by the Assistant Director but if possible I wanted their full, not nominal, co-operation. Many fears were expressed by them about being 'represented' through me, and about whether the Assistant Director would have privileged access to the research findings and there were attempts to influence or control the research methods used.

A request was made by the educational psychologists that I should put my proposals on paper, prior to discussion. I had to convince them of several things: my neutrality, my integrity, and my unwillingness to be unduly influenced by others. The brief proposals which I prepared for them later proved invaluable as an entry ticket and sent conviction to personal approaches. I loaned a copy to the Assistant Director, whom I was keeping informed of progress, so that suspicions about secrecy were unlikely to grow.

When I had finished interviewing the educational psychologists, I began the parental interviews that had by now been set up. These were finished in November. I had intended to interview schools next, but there was a national strike which was not yet resolved. Moreover, I knew that it would not be fruitful to try to contact schools so near to Christmas and so I turned to Social Services. Support from upper management, made at my request, gave official backing for a direct approach to be made to each of the area teams. I also obtained the support of a key figure in Social Services who helped the process of identifying area team social workers to be interviewed for my sample. I did not have to persuade social workers of the relevance of my research, as there had been considerable frustration with the new procedures for assessment. No one refused, despite work pressures. My last interview was with the Chief Fieldwork Services Officer, in order to obtain an intermanagerial perspective.

The most difficult group to approach directly and persuade were the mainstream school staff. I knew from experience that Headteachers would make individual and arbitrary decisions about whether they would allow someone to interview staff. So I decided on a personal approach to each one in my sample. Often I was obliged to interview the Headteacher, both to identify a key person, and to gain consent to interview them. I had just two school staff refusals: one because of staffing shortages, the other maintaining that they didn't have a problem with special needs in the school. Last of all, I interviewed all those in the office responsible for carrying out the process of assessment. The final interview was with the Assistant Director for Special Education. It seemed as though after a certain point, there was a snowballing effect, rather like organising a party to which you know that a number of guests will come, if key guests have agreed. Eventually more than 50 interviews were carried out.

Learning from Practitioner Research: Improving Practice

In my research role, I was able to listen to parents from a more neutral position. I was forced to take account of the frequently repeated tale of not being listened to by 'official' people. I began to recognise that these were not isolated incidents, but a pattern that required explanation, and I gradually realised the extent to which I had managed to discount such complaints in the past, as if I had been able to develop professional ear-muffs. Unerringly, the parents whom I had interviewed used the language of power and powerlessness to describe their experiences. I had to conclude that poor professional listening might also be a means of exercising and maintaining professional power at their expense.

The spin-off from this was that I began to listen more accurately to parents in my professional role. I had just started a parents' self-help group at the special school at which I worked. Then two events happened in quick succession: the election of parent governors which was for many parents a first 'political' activity; followed by an attempt by the councillors to change the name of the school, which failed because parents used their newly found political confidence to write letters of protest at the inept choice. The increasing confidence of the parents had positive spin-offs on the children at the school, but organised parental opposition was not very endearing to councillors who had been thwarted.

Did this account for the proposal to relocate my post? Or was the authority beginning to grow alarmed at what my research might have uncovered? It will always be a matter of conjecture. What did I unearth? In terms of the Local Authority, minor embarrassments of bureaucratic incompetence, and authoritarian and impersonal communication. It was hardly a matter to bring down governments! There were the usual organisational and communication problems, and human beings struggling with poorly devised systems over which they had little control. There were some surprises in the way in which decisions were made in the assessment process: things are often not what they seem when it comes to decision-making. There is a well-rehearsed notion that someone, somewhere, makes a rational decision based on facts, which often proves to be a myth. The research findings were written up with a storm cloud gathering over my head.

A Cautionary Ending

Three months after I handed in my research thesis, I handed in my resignation, having fought a losing battle against relocation. My offer to discuss my findings was not taken up. At the very least, I could have given the Local Authority considerable assistance in rewording their very brusque communications to parents! The research was published. Soon after, in a *Times Educational Supplement* article on the research, the journalist succeeded in identifying the Local Authority involved, and a spokesman for the authority's Education Department was quoted as saying that 'he hadn't yet seen my report'.

An Agenda for Practitioner Research

COLIN FLETCHER

I would like to develop this chapter through connections rather than contentions, through display rather than debate. There are matters within practitioner research to address first and then the task of relating practitioner research to post-qualifying training can be tried with more confidence.

The Development of Practitioner Research

The practitioner's 'practice wisdom', upon which so much depends, cannot be assumed or comfortably taken for granted. There are problems about what it means, where it comes from, its durability and mutability.

For De Roos (1990) 'Practice wisdom is a basic element of social work...practice wisdom is developed through the subjective experience of everyday life and actual practice in social work'.

A dictionary meaning of these words says that wisdom is the opposite to folly. It is 'the capacity of judging rightly in matters relating to life and conduct' (OED). There is a soundness to judgement and, by implication, dignity and respect, discretion and spiritual perception. When personified, wisdom is almost always feminine.

Responsible practice makes the bridge from knowledge to wisdom. Practice is engaging in methods of action and can produce occupational habits and customs. Practice, at times, can cloud our vision, wisdom always can cleanse it. There is a balanced tension between the strengths of wisdom and the weaknesses of practice. In addition there are the positive strengths of practice.

De Roos (1990) is concerned to present the theories which support 'practice wisdom'. These are:

1. Herbert Simon on bounded reality[1]
2. Donald Campbell on evolutionary epistemology[2]
3. Donald Schon on reflexive practice[3]

Gould (1989) is also impressed by the work of Donald Schon (1987) particularly the refinement of practice wisdom as 'reflection-in-action'. Gould sees parallels between Schon's ideas and those of Kelly (1955), his meta psychology of personal construct theory.

The more radical aspect of Schon's ideas is that a theory used in practice is practitioner-led, it is implicit and developed through experiential learning. It is exciting and thought-provoking to follow the development of Schon's ideas, their influence and their parallels. These ideas are finding considerable significance in the professions of teaching, nursing and planning too.

Meanwhile in social work, 'practice-wisdom' refers to some habits currently engendered both by oppressive enquiry and by engrossment in rapid change. What may have been long taken for granted may be marooned in nostalgia now. Rapid change, against the insights of practice wisdom, may also fail to attract the intellectual and emotional energy which the engendering of `new' practice wisdom seems to require.

My impression is that practice wisdom is remarkably tough. But I am deeply troubled when those in whom it resides resign. There are important empirical and academic questions about the transfer of practice wisdom from one generation to the next and the persistence of practice wisdom in hostile conditions.

For the first part of this chapter I shall base the agenda items on a belief that practice wisdom in social work will continue to be dependable and durable albeit, most regrettably, under duress.

The Question of Problems and Questions

Whitaker and Archer (1989) in their thorough and helpful book *Research by Social Workers* write that:

> *...formulating research purposes is done step by step, starting from an interest in some practice issue; restating the interest in the form of a question which represents one's overall purpose; judging whether the practice interest is a researchable issue and, if it is not, abandoning or restating it; making existing practice wisdom explicit and examining the relevant literature and `unpacking' the generally stated overall research purpose by specifying the sub-purposes contained within it (p.35).*

Their chapter 'Formulating Research Purposes' skilfully 'elaborates these points. So, too, it is generally true that practitioners often have a burning issue from which to begin. Yet they are also interested in what kind of study they are doing and benefit from modelling their study on the successes of earlier students. In the opening chapter two sets or kinds of typologies of practitioner research were given. The `types' can now be related to their distinctive outcomes (please see Table 1).

The scope is to begin from any field, mental health, child care or the elderly for example, and to express a purpose from each column. There are 16 alternatives!

Table 1
The Scope and Alternatives of Practitioner Research

Realities Studied	*Resulting Recommendations*
State of the art surveys	Action plans
Investigations	Awareness programmes
Appraisals	Advocacy
Innovations	Accountability

Each alternative has its own style or at least some distinguishing features - though there is not yet the systematic evidence to prove this assertion. What there is suggests as much though. In the lists of current projects there is a bewildering problem of choice for those about to make their own (see Whitaker and Archer, 1989, p.7). Cranfield's list also has the look of a brightly illuminated Christmas tree about it (see Appendix One).

It is probably true that prospective practitioner-researchers find more inspiration in Table 2 than in Table 1. They say things like 'I can find myself in these, there is scope for me, I don't feel odd anymore, I can add myself to this lot without feeling conspicuous!'.

The Question of Appreciating Practitioner Research Processes

Any research can be a lonely activity. Yet practitioner research has three ways in which those times which are solitary can be experienced to good effect. First those who 'have been through the mill' can speak about their 'coping strategies'. Secondly those currently engaged can share their feelings. Thirdly a practitioner research project can be shared between two or more participants. Whitaker and Archer (1989, p.105) say:

> *For practitioner-researchers to talk over their experiences with others also doing their own research helps considerably both with the task itself and in removing blocks to progress. Participants in Cranfield's courses for experienced social workers benefited from the searching questions and interests of others. By observing the work and struggles of others with diverse practice interests, each course member became familiar with a range of research designs and strategies appropriate to those interests.*

The value of collective enquiry and constructive criticism may be rather obvious . Less obvious, though, is the form which searching questions may take (see Table 2).

Conflict occurs when two practitioners want to research together as part of post-qualifying education. I have personal experience of having encouraged co-researching for an MPhil, omitted to support the process (excused by other 'pressures'),

Table 2
A Self-Help and Mutual Help Questionnaire on Practitioner Research

1. **What is the question for me:**
   • as a person with values?
   • as a professional with responsibilities?
   • as a post-holder with problems?
   • as a 'doer' with processes?

2. **What fieldwork approaches:**
   • couldn't I do?
   • would I not do?
   • would like to do?
   • can I find out about?

3. **What are the likely fieldwork experiences of**
   • getting started?
   • getting involved (who's doing the talking)?
   • counselling?
   • upsets and delays?
   • moving a mountain of data?

4. **What are the probable issues of making sense?**
   • because of the form of data
   • connecting with ideas, concepts and theories?
   • the importance of acknowledging thinkers?
   • with my peers?

5. **What trouble can happen**
   • confirming discomforts?
   • disconfirming truths?
   • advancing an argument and recommendations?
   • being overtaken by events?

fudging the paperwork and then forcing the award through when an outstanding single thesis was accredited by its (their) external examiner. In retrospect my part in this history was a rather shabby and shamefaced History was made through two shared 'her stories'. Even so I was pleased and glad that Cranfield could countenance the precedent at all (Please see the extracts from Phillipson's and Riley's account in Table 3).

The Question of Competences for Practitioner Research

Table 2, by implication, also relates to the skills and attitudes which the practitioner-researcher may expect to develop: personal, methodological, intellectual and interpersonal. Each question on opens up lines of anticipated experience along which there will be realisations and resistances.

The aspiration to do practitioner research has to be strong

Table 3
Co-Working as an Academic Conflict

Extracts from Julia Phillipson and Maggie Riley (1990)

In his brief discussion of the 'ideological clash between the normal university requirement for (such) research to be the candidate's original work, and the ideals of the co-operative paradigm' Peter Reason (1988) describes the 'problem' as 'surmountable' in practice because the student can be seen as the 'primary researcher', and can write their view 'in some form of consultation with members of the group'. But what are two students supposed to do? (or three, or thirty?) Must responsibility always be broken down into little pieces that can be nailed on individuals?

To suggest - or indeed insist - that the 'rules' mean that we must publicly deny the fact that this work is intrinsically a joint production - though we are separate and different people with separate voices - and is owned equally by both of us together with the women who speak through it - is to invalidate process and to lie (p.21).

One of the most precious gifts we were given during our journey of co-research was that of seeing and using storytelling as a powerful and expressive means of learning, of making sense, which goes deeper than simple explanation and which has much to contribute to the research process, as it does to other ways of learning. It is a 'method' which women and children have often used in trying to express their experience, particularly of violence when they are afraid of what will happen to them if they speak the truth directly (p.210).

In an award by research thesis course, the 'ownership and originality' issues are not actually confronted until the end, because accreditation is entirely 'product' focused - it is concerned only with assessing a thesis end-product and not the process of researching as it is happening (p.216).

...co-researching, like co-training is probably more time consuming than working alone. But it has not been lonely in the 'Protestant's sense of inner loneliness' that David Morgan (1981, pp.105, 109) describes in his discussion of the 'masculine culture of academic life' and its effect on research practice, the 'unseen side of the male academic culture'. In the light of feminist understanding, Morgan argues the need for male researchers to look 'more critically or reflectively' at their own institutions of higher education (p.230). Maybe Academia needs to consider that common working is not a 'subsidiary' tradition but rather what Joanna Russ (1983) would call a parallel one (p.235).

---

enough to overcome obstacles. Indeed the path is strewn with boulders and beset with big holes! When people finish they usually say 'well, I did it, I've learned a lot and I'm going to take a good break before attempting something else'. The preceding chapter looks at the longer term personal and professional significances in some detail. Those recently completing write about what they have learned with statements such as:

• One does not need large groups of subjects.
• I began to understand the process of structuring a design.

- I have learned a more ordered way of looking at my work.
- It has given me new ideas for my new post.
- I feel keener to examine processes and share them.
- I'm less inclined to 'accept' without questioning.
- I seem to be finding many researchable questions in my work.

(all taken from Whitaker and Archer, 1989, pp.103-104)

Perhaps these expressions in some way meet the more formal and abstract requirements for the Research Area of CCETSW's framework (see Table 4). To be sure, CCETSW expresses the view that

Although the competence requirements may imply discrete areas of activity this is only a device to assist assessment processes...the statements may need adding to or amending.

What CCETSW calls 'practice research' seems more formal than the research statements given a little earlier, those convey an impression of practitioners taking some zest from the rind of research. Compatibility is desirable between expectations and expressions: the requirements could move towards being more 'practitioner-friendly'.

The Question of Guidance for Practitioner Research

Over time I have felt unsure being described as a tutor or as a supervisor. To come back to first principles again: there is a partnership between the professional autonomy of the practitioner and the professional authority of the tutor or supervisor. Tutor refers to the one-to-one personal aspect and supervisor refers to the better overall vision which the guide should have. So far so good, but what would be a good title for the 'teacher' and why?

CCETSW has settled upon a 'consultant' as being the word to describe being responsible 'for overseeing and directing a candidate's work'. And so:

Candidates being assessed in the area of research will require support and guidance of a consultant, whereas, candidates who are developing advanced practice skills will require a mentor (p.40).

Seeking the help of dictionaries once more I learn that:

Mentor: an experienced and trusted counsellor, an adviser (OED). *whilst*

Consultant: a person qualified to give professional advice or services, an adviser (OED)
one who gives professional advice (Chambers).

Table 4
CCETSW (1990:38) Competence Requirements for the
Research Area of Post-Qualifying Education and Training

Practice Researchers Must
(i)   Be able to critically evaluate different types of research, research
        design, data collection and analysis and be able to use information
        technology. This must include understanding what can and cannot
        be achieved through research.
(ii)   Be able to identify and set out in accessible form the knowledge
        base relevant to an issue to be investigated through research
        including material from both within and outwith the UK.
(iii)   Be able to manage and carry out systematic research from the
        specification of purposes through to and including the preparation
        of a full written report. This must include:
        (a)   identifying the relevance of research to practice and\or
                  policy;
        (b)   being able to identify and work around obstacles which may
                  arise in their research.
(iv)   Be able to articulate the values which are influencing and
        informing their research. This must include:
        (a)   conducting their research in an anti-racist and anti-
                  discriminatory manner;
        (b)   analysing the impact of different perceptions, bias and
                  prejudice in research and design and taking account of them
                  when planning or conducting research;
        (c)   acknowledging their own expectations and preferences with
                  respect to outcomes and conclusions and taking these into
                  account when planning and analysing research material.
(v)   Have skills in making research and research activity relevant to
        practice and usable by service-delivery organisations. This must
        include:
        (a)   engaging and communicating with colleagues within the
                  organisation and to diverse groups including, where relevant,
                  other professions and consumers of personal Social Services,
                  the results or consequences of research;
        (b)   being able to articulate the processes of managing research;
        (c)   being able to assist others in the use of rigorous methods to
                  evaluate the consequences of their practice.

I can but hope that whatever distinctions there may be actually
blur, leaving the best of both behind: experienced; trustworthy;
wise, professional advice.

There is a deeper current here, too. Experience tells me that
guidance goes through stages and a key part of this agenda is to
suggest that in a learning partnership there are these stages of
fruitful friction.

The way is made up of four stages

- *Beginning the research and developing its purposes*
  When the practitioner's wishes prevail until, through debate, tutor and practitioner are mutually clear.
- *Designing the fieldwork*
  When the tutor's wishes prevail until, through 'test and try', the data sought is recognised by both to be meaningful.
- *Making the analysis*
  When practitioner and tutor are separate but overlap and each is offering interpretations.
- *Making the account*
  When practitioner and tutor separate, the tutor being a 'first but equal' critic.

So it is only at one stage, fieldwork design, that the tutor's professional advice may be properly dominant.

Failing these stages of 'alternating leadership', with both a camaraderie and a considerate conflict either the tutor can take over or the practitioner can break free and lose any hope of help. Very little is known about the consulting room - any consulting room (cf Fletcher, 1973) - clearly more will need to be known and openly shared.

All of this, too, is on the person-to-person model. A further sphere of learning lies in the guidance of co-working practitioner workers. Speaking from their own experience, Phillipson and Riley ask:

> *Maybe joint researchers should have joint supervisors for joint supervision?*

However technically expressed, mutual respect and companionship enable the development of competences.

In time, and because of my background in education, I have come to suggest that the partnership has such potential for equality that we can speak of 'teacher-learners' and 'learner-teachers'. I am not trying to pretend that the person with an academic position will not be assumed to be superior in some sense. Instead, I want to underline the amount of learning any tutor does in practitioner research and, of course, the amount of teaching which any practitioner is likely to do too.

Guidance from the tutor is particularly appropriate when 'unpacking' the answers to the self-help and mutual help questionnaire in Table 2. In education, the case for cooperation between parents and teachers as two equal adults with responsibilities for particular children rests upon the tangents they take towards each others' expertise: parents know their child in great detail (teachers do not); teachers know the characteristics of an age group (parents seldom do) (Stacey, 1991).

Is it me or does everybody do this?

asks the practitioner-researcher. Back comes the reply:

It is you and everybody does that.

To anticipate exchanges like this, there is coursework. A group of tutors taking turns to give their own perspective prevents needless repetition and shares out the responsibility, a little, for each student. 'Not individual property but collective responsibility' seems a useful maxim for teaching groups. Whitaker and Archer (1989) have also given some thought to 'structures and schemes to learn the craft and develop practice-based research' (pp.109-112).

Great strides have been made since the 'bad old days' when methods meant 'doing statistics'. Somewhat smaller steps have been taken over guidance in relation to theory. Practitioners theorise whilst doing research. Not surprisingly they seek or stumble upon difficulties in explaining *why* things happen the way they did. Organisational structures keep getting into the act. As Charkin (1986) found in her survey, the more formal and centralised the agency the less it is likely to use research, any research. Necessary guidance includes some organisational theory and understanding of social institutions.

Beyond this organisational context, there is more theorising which the practitioner-researcher is called upon to do. Guidance with theorising, as with methods, becomes eclectic. Berman-Rossi's (1988) survey suggests that teachers in schools of social work cluster around two major traditions: pragmatist and rationalist-empiricist. The demands of practitioner research do tend to attract pragmatists and to antagonise empiricists.

As Goldstein (1990) says if the need for a theoretical base is aligned with the development of practice-wisdom then a whole range of generative and humanistic theories come into view. Narrative Theory, Social Constructionism, Cognitive Theory and Feministic Theory are four peaks on this extensive range. When these peaks are approached the practitioner may want to work in great detail with relatively little data. Jones (1990) discusses a twenty minute transcript from a three hour interview with a social worker. His 'interpretive strategies' include sociological, educational, feministic and literary theory. It is fair to say that he was guided in this direction. Practitioner research appears to encourage the eclectic and normative qualities in the guide. There is both a liberal tolerance and a liberationary task in guidance.

How Is Practitioner Research Related to Agencies?

Not every agency may be committed to a liberal tolerance and a liberationary task. As with the earlier contrast between competences and what practitioner-researchers said they had learned there is some distance between the technical expectations and where the practitioner may feel that the 'real' problems and potentials actually lie.

In its advanced level competences CCETSW (1990) requires the practitioner to be able to:

...make a significant contribution to the development, delivery and evaluation of the service provided in a chosen area.

and

...identify and analyse trends and initial strategies for change in their own work, their agency and professional networks (Summary).

A balance needs to be reached between seeking these competences as direct benefits and paying the costs of doing so. Whitaker and Archer, devote a chapter to the costs and benefits for all concerned; practitioner; agency; colleagues and clients (1989, pp.103-108), a chapter which has outstanding integrity.

The point here is that the balance may only be achieved by a mature three-way contract between academe, agency and practitioner. One recent contract read as follows:

- The project will respect and make use of knowledge already available in the service.
- A participative approach will be adopted.
- Initiatives will aim to be examples of good practice.
- There will be regular feedback.
- Data sought will be relevant to effecting positive change.
- Imaginative responses will be networked.

The drafting of contracts like this could help to restrain the dominance and diffidence which both agencies and academics are prone to adopt.

The terms of such a contract are meant to keep the formality of the agency - academic relationship down to a minimum. Gelman and Wardell's findings (1988) suggest why this should be so:

The more explicit the curriculum policy statement and accreditation standards become in relation to the field component of the curriculum the closer and more complex becomes the relationship between educational institutions and the practice community. [The more complexity the more formality]. Such formality has the potential for strengthening the field-agency relationship or destroying it.

Preston's experience of contracts is more positive.

Contracts offer the opportunity to discuss and resolve clashes in perspective by giving each party a change to negotiate the nature of the intervention and a role or choice in the decision-making process (Preston, 1989, p.5).

If agencies are reluctant to express their interests in a contract they may have in mind more of a 'sponsorship' model - no deviations, no debate and no diatribes about abusers of power!

Sponsorship rarely 'works' for practitioner research. It is far better for the practitioner to have the idea and the agency to acknowledge and support the intended research. Practitioner research generally fails otherwise. Only extreme perseverance can overcome an agency's interference, insistence or indifference, as Nicki Cornwell's experience shows.

How Significant Is Practitioner Research?

It is usually possible to counter difficult questions by saying 'I don't know, there's not enough evidence yet'. Practitioner research could easily be defended by such as tactic. Yet to do so would be out of character and a refusal to read the signs which can be seen already.

Because practitioner research is not theory - led there may never be an overall analysis of 'the' field. And if the sequence between knowledge and practice is cyclical rather than serial (a rhythm of tides rather than a running against the clock, Howe, 1965, pp.154-155) then as practice is made explicit the explicitness will confirm some parts and challenge others. The cyclical, contingent relationship can be very satisfying to the practitioner but it does make the imposition of meanings invalid and it does make a mockery of authoritarian control.

Another limitation is that of there being endless case-studies often taking place simultaneously. It is quite likely that up and down the country, any country, lots of practitioners have the same idea. As they are primarily concerned to relate with life *in* their own agency such 'repetitions' are probably fine by them. But I can imagine that they may be thought inefficient by agency managers who could then try to rationalise the endeavours.

A still greater limitation may derive from the language used regularly in practitioner research. It is the language of issues, forces, choices and dilemmas. Some will find this language combative or at the very least discomforting. Some will want answers rather than choices, decisions rather than dilemmas. This is the language which aspires to looking at reality squarely, even holistically. Part of an agenda is to work out what these and related terms mean, where and how they differ from the language of business. An adjacent agenda item is how to secure an acceptance of its appropriateness to practitioner research when it obviously conveys an impression of widespread friction.

How Can Practitioner Research Influence Initial Training?

Coming after comments on the limitations the answer to this section's question can only be moderate and modest. Those who teach practice or research are usually at the bottom of the pecking order (Hartmann, 1990). Also, according to Staub (1988): 'There continues to be a gender-based division between male - theoreticians and the female practitioners'. So, too, the theory-practice debate contains at least three positions:

...good practice is best informed by a broad grasp of theoretical principles (Sowers and Thyer, 1985; Rumgay, 1988).

...a middle range conceptualisation that works both deductively from conceptual models and inductively from practice experiences (Teiglser and Chambon, 1989).

...the student should define problems interactionally. The instructor should help students to explore that which is less known, less developed, less structures and less certain (Gilterman, 1988).

If at all, practitioner research will find favour with the latter two and less prestigious points of view.

Where this happens initial training research projects may take the same titles as post-qualifying projects but with less detail and for a shorter distance. Case studies, especially critical incidents, offer a 'natural focus' for realising, the practice wisdom, the issues and the dilemmas. Davies and Reid (1988) put forward the term 'event analysis' to describe the approach which they have established at San Diego:

All types of clinical events begin characteristically with a marker that the client system is ready to tackle a certain issue, followed by a particular intervention and immediate client response that bring that event to a close. From systematic analysis of informative events, ideas are gained about the workings of specific methods of a treatment model, its apparent effectiveness, promising innovations, limitations etc. Event analysis points to where changes are needed and thus serves as a bridge between research and practice (Abstract).

It is possible that event analysis has similarities to role-play - both ask students to get into real situations. Yet it is the practicum, (or practice curriculum or placement) which offers practitioner research possibilities in new and distinctive ways. If post-qualifying education is to suggest a shape it is that initial students take a procedure in depth, ask how it could be improved and answer questions about *their own* learning.

Conclusion

How far do the articles in this book serve as models which can be used in initial training? As the starting point for practitioner research is professional experience the question may seem to give rise to the answer that without such experience then only the mechanics of method such as styles of survey and appraisals may be appropriate. But two further possibilities exist which could align practitioner research with an initial training project. The first is to research what practitioners say are the 'hot topics', the puzzles they would like to unravel if they had the time to 'stand back and reflect'. The second is to tackle 'as-if' questions. For example is there a `best demonstrated practice' in a chosen social work area, who might know, how could it be discovered and described, what `blue prints' would that offer those who might aspire to such excellence themselves? 'Peer affirmation' is the key to access 'best demonstrated practice', the credibility and standing of some social workers managers and directors is a pathway to where a great deal can to be learned - 'if one has the ears to hear'.

The second approach has been popular in private sector studies and takes the form of shadowing experts. This must be an unsettling experience most of the time and on occasions mutually unnerving (albeit that a discrete distance can be maintained through 'diary keeping'). So, too, `shadowing' and `mentoring', may blur into each other as they do in articled teacher training. The exploration of expertise is fraught with problems of exposure and emotional exploitation. Nevertheless learning through 'as if' questions is engaging with the trials and trends as they are appreciated by the 'best-practitioners'. It involves 'taking the role of the other': asking if I were in their shoes what would I do; if that were to be done what would probably happen next; what mistakes have been avoided by that course of action and why is that outcome considered 'better than average'? Most significantly of all, perhaps, how can the fog of thinking 'its all down to personalities' be cleared without losing the salience of the personal gifts and touch?

In initial teacher training the debate over these matters is extensive and often acrimonious (Grimmett, 1989; Shon, 1977). There are those for whom practitioner research represents an 'apolitical action research', for whom the collective struggle of teachers (or social workers) is far more important than the competences of specific professionals (Adelman, 1991). There are others who think that initial training *is* more about skills rather than the subtleties of consciousness and that skills should be learned first - judgements later. For the latter, practitioner research is a circle which cannot be squared. They would reject a priority upon either practitioner - defined problems or 'best demonstrated practice' studies. Rather, for them, there are academic issues of investigating care and client, comparison and control and rigorous research methods to be learned in order to do so. The differences of opinion reach right back to whether there are theories *of* practice or theories *in* practice, or, more radically, both.

A unified pathway is still a long way off and this makes the destination of practitioner research very far off indeed. Shari and Bushe (1987) write of a 'visionary action research' one which 'creates visions and explores the situational characteristics that must be incorporated into the organisation's vision'. Practitioner-researchers, though, know that their enthusiasm is but one part of the equation, they acknowledge there are also factors based on clients, agency and the politics of the day.

A mature relationship with such politics involves working through the complexities of practitioner-researcher's realism, that:

- clients are citizens first
- practitioners are citizens too
- agencies are agents not ultimate authorities
- legislation spurs the development of new trends.

Whether it be in relation to the Children Act 1989 in the UK or Public Law 99-457 in the US (Radin, 1989), the destination of practitioner research is to spell out the future options for practice with the attendant arguments for or against. Political will makes the choices. Practitioner research helps to spell out those options, those choices.

The Significances of Practitioner Research

BOB BROAD

What happened to the research contained in this book? We, as editors, had questions about what had been the significance, of the research to the practitioner-researchers themselves; to their role and ways of working; to the departments and organisations in which they worked; elsewhere both at national level and beyond? We wished to know what were the problems which were encountered as well as other opportunities which were created directly or indirectly as a result of the research.

The best way to answer these questions was to write direct to all of the contributors rather than 'second guess' the answers ourselves. Given that some of the research studies in this book go back some years (although significantly the findings still feel fresh and relevant) it was inevitable that not all the contributors would or could reply by the deadline. However the majority, nine, did manage it, with their replies varying in length between 500 and 5,000 words. Whilst it is not claimed their views are representative of all Cranfield practitioner social work research students, it is argued that their responses enabled a series of professional and social policy themes to be identified. A further advantage of analysing pieces drawn from a period spanning several years is that it is possible to draw out the changing professional, policy and political agenda. Those issues concerned with the changing research agenda of the 1980s and 1990s, at least so far as practitioner social work research is concerned, will be outlined at the end of this chapter. It begins by looking at the significance of the research as detailed by the book's contributors, under specific headings. These include the significance of the research to the person completing the research, their role, the significance to the department in which they returned to work and the significance of organisational resistance. Within each of these sub-headings are identifiable quotations which can be readily related back to the relevant chapter.

Significance to the Person

A considerable amount of energy and commitment went into undertaking the practitioner research, the completion of which had an impact on them as a person. For me, without a shadow of a doubt, it gave me the confidence to go on to study for a doctorate and complete other pieces of research. For others experiences varied.

We are both conscious that we use a lot of the ideas and theories, both those discovered and those we created, in other settings with women in addition to working with managers...Experience and learning from it (i.e. Cranfield) has been invaluable in being able to offer a student daughter extra tutorials in writing about feminist and other approaches to research (Maggie Riley and Julia Phillipson).

It has taught me there is no substitute for asking questions and analysing the answers (David Bowen).

It is pleasing to note that most of the issues recommended as a result of the research findings have now been addressed. For me, personally, this is very rewarding (Eric Knapman).

Well intellectually equipped social workers are an asset to their employers. They have the ability to question poor procedures, bad working practices, and the ability to research into issues that may improve the quality of social work practice (Grace Thomas).

The experience of carrying out the research remains with me constantly. My previous education had left me with a rag bag of knowledge and frameworks which made it difficult to get a consistent view of the world...The act of carrying out practitioner research forced me to construct a methodological framework which would give a coherent perspective. This was the hardest part of the process and the aspect that has made the most lasting impact (Simon Villette).

The research has been of great value...I have established a relevant model for work with families of children with disabilities which realistically identifies the processes experienced by parents....On many occasions the model has been verified by parents of older children who are able to take stock of their experiences...The organisation probably appointed me partly...because of the significance of the research to this particular area of work (Anthea Coghlan).

Undertaking the research also had a profound and lasting effect on people's ways of working and thinking and tackling issues at the workplace. For example my 'changes checklist' form of assessment was subsequently used by local community services teams to assess staff expectations of change and then actual client change.

Significance to Ways of Working and Role

Having successfully challenged the 'rules' in higher education, we have been able to encourage others and see co-working as a valid stance to take and to share our experiences and understanding of the conflicts, contradictions and supportiveness of doing it that way (Maggie Riley and Julia Phillipson)

Now I realise that once the discipline of enquiry into issues has been implanted in my mind, it is easy to find a research subject in every aspect of the work we do ... I questioned what I viewed as bad practices and challenged attitudes about racism in services delivered to the ethnic minority users in the team (Grace Thomas).

I started thinking about ...professional power...If you expect qualifying students to demonstrate anti-discriminatory and anti-racist practice (and CCETSW does) then I couldn't ask them to do something I wouldn't do myself...so I started asking questions about the implementation of equal opportunity policies in the university (Nikki Cornwall).

Having spent two years considering the educational effects of making care orders in respect of children who had not attended school regularly, I found myself morally committed to act upon my own findings. The conclusion that making care orders in such circumstances had no positive effect, meant that I had to change my working practices...In the longer term the experience of supervised practitioner research has had significant effects on my working. I am more confident in the interpretation of research findings...It has enabled to make better use (as a manager) of statistical information and not to be afraid of numbers (David Bowen).

The completion of the research did not only have an impact at a personal level in terms of personal satisfaction and changed and more questioning ways of working. In some cases the significance of the research was extended beyond the individual and their role to that of the department.

Significance to the Department

Critical analysis of the role of the personal tutor in social work education...has stimulated a fundamental reappraisal of tutoring / studies advice throughout professional and academic departments within the University of Ulster (David Bamford).

The conclusion of my research was that making care orders...had no positive educational effect. It would have been indefensible to continue with a procedure which I knew would not have the intended effect. Because of my position at the head of a Local Authority's educational welfare service, I was able to apply that decision immediately. That the conclusion had been reached through practitioner research at a reputable academic institution gave added authority to my changed policy. Assertion was, however, not enough. The research had to be presented to colleagues in seminars and by making the text available (David Bowen).

My own research...proved very helpful to alert staff to the possibility that their own professional background could have a very significant, if not always appropriate, impact on the assessment of 'user needs' ...I was also able to establish monitoring systems to ensure a greater sense of objectivity was applied to the assessment process (Mike Carpenter).

At one point the Social Services department was considering its policy towards managing the 'heavy end' of the delinquency market and an assistant director discussed my research with me. At the time consideration was being given to re-opening a similar centre. My recommendation was that they should not, but if they needed the facilities they should be part of a much larger institution. This would give a better chance of stability and lead to less conflict amongst the staff members. Since then the remand and more general 'holding' function served by the centre has transferred to another, much larger, institution in the county. I don't know if my research or comments had any influence...I suspect my comments merely confirmed decisions which had already been taken for other more practical reasons such as spare accommodation and surplus staffing (Simon Villette).

Some of the recommendations in my research have now been applied and every probation officer in this county has a checklist on which they are required to identify the factors which contribute to offending behaviour and alcohol tops the list...The service has provided training for officers and facilitates alcohol education for offenders as part of our general approach to their behaviour (Eric Knapman).

It has been necessary to continue 'evangelising' about the findings of the research because even my immediate colleagues tend to use more conventional (and less useful) models of intervention with children and their families. I am confident that...there will be opportunities to build on the findings of the research (Anthea Coghlan).

A number of contributors considered that the research was significant beyond their immediate environment, for some partly because of the organisational resistance they encountered, but for others because of the universality of their ideas and the passion which informed them.

Significance in Other Spheres

Kernels of ideas eventually became research projects and papers which in some cases reached national audiences.

The findings also formed a paper at a national conference of chief education social workers. Through that, and a subsequent conference which concentrated on a part of the research, it had I believe some influence on the working practices of my peers elsewhere in the country (David Bowen).

Through the sales of the book publication Personal Tutor in Social Work Education *this research...has stimulated significant critical analyses in other institutions throughout the British Isles which offer courses, which include a significant tutorial function...This research is now between 8 and 10 years old but...it has come to be regarded within the British Isles as the standard work on social work tutoring...used as a reference point not least by CCETSW...The research has also attracted significant interest in North America (David Bamford).*

On a wider scale it would be inappropriate to claim success for the research as it was sharply focused to the way that Northamptonshire reacted to the problem. However nationally the uncertainty which the Probation Service had about coping with problem drinkers in the late 1970s and early 1980s [Knapman is referring here to probation clients - editors], has to a large degree, been overcome and activity in this area is much more widespread (Eric Knapman).

My enthusiasm for the separation of the roles (of assessing and providing Social Services) has been satisfied with the introduction of purchaser and provider in the new organisation of social care services...This new process reinforces the importance of the opinion of the service users in choosing the type of help most suited to their own situation. The assessor or care manager can limit their responsibility to assessing service needs and commissioning the specific help agreed with users. I wish I could take credit for the change at national level but I have to limit my contribution to that of identifying the problem and seeking to minimise its impact by heightening awareness and supervising practice (Mike Carpenter).

In relation to the wider application of ideas with other organisations:

We have a sense of now having a wider base of theory and ideas for our practice as trainers and consultants working with both men and women ... An example of that would be (Maggie) working with a group of leisure services team managers - predominantly male - and exploring ideas about power and empowerment within them in a similar way to that we developed on the woman and management programmes (Maggie Riley and Julia Phillipson).

Again the same authors write of another sphere of significance namely that of developing and confirming theory and values here about feminist approaches.

Our experience since the Cranfield work has further confirmed and clarified the value of feminist approaches both to research and to organisational development ... Our version of practitioner research means we have an alternative model to offer in discussion with others interested in or undertaking a range of formal or informal research endeavours (Maggie Riley and Julia Phillipson).

For another researcher the impact of the research was less certain.

...it is possible that further examination of some of the findings within the research could throw light on the nature of potential models for parent/professional relationships and it may also help to identify ways of relating in the context of family pathologies (Anthea Coghlan).

The process of concentrated study and the raising of

expectations, confidence and skills sometimes produced difficulties of role readjustment or role dissonance. It is understandable that having completed this research those who were 'staff' felt that they had increased knowledge and commitment to research and improving practice, but that they were not necessarily in a strong position or a high enough grade to influence policy. Additionally there is the remaining issue of whether the organisation was a 'learning organisation' open to fresh ideas. Indeed I can recall returning to my employer in 1982 and being told 'you are not employed here as a researcher' when wanting to investigate possible racist practice by probation officers concerning referrals to an employment project. Subsequently, in fact, I continued the research which in any case was already well under way. Those findings helped me, as personnel manager, overseeing referrals at the time, to adopt a more consistent and anti-discriminatory approach to all black and white offenders and ex-offenders referred to the employment project.[1] At that stage, in 1982, my then employing organisation, as I am sure with others, was simply not willing to see or acknowledge that there could be racist practices which must be challenged as of right. The position ten years on (at the time of writing) is much improved and changed, but in patches.[2]

Significance of Organisational Resistance

In this section on organisational resistance, it has been decided to include lengthy quotations from Grace Thomas because of the scale of the difficulties she faced upon her return to work, and subsequently in other work places.

Looking back to my first two years as a practitioner (after Cranfield) my assessment is that the burning flames of enthusiasm and an inquisitive mind was still alive in me, but the yearning to keep the fire burning was gradually becoming a struggle...(At a new workplace on the first day) The boss told me bluntly that people who have two or three degrees don't usually make good social workers and that she hoped it would not be so in my case...Despite every attempt to knock the daylight out of my soul, my inquisitive mind did not rest...My personal experience and my observations are that there are too many factors which are disabling to the intellect of any aspiring practitioners who may wish to consider research into any area of social work at the work area...Instead of Social Services becoming fertile grounds for conceiving practitioner research, such places observed the obituary of research ideas and academic consideration gets lost...At Local Authority offices where racial, intellectual and prejudices of minority groups are rife...places like that are hardly breeding grounds for conceiving intellectual progress and practitioner research (Grace Thomas).

Whilst we continue to be convinced...of the value of women only programmes, there has been very little movement by organisations in promoting similar development opportunities for male managers and mixed management groups as part of a...strategy aimed at changing the culture (Maggie Riley and Julia Phillipson).

(One) employer, despite having seconded me for the period of study, had not developed a policy for providing services for these children and I found a frustrating lack of commitment to using the findings of the research in either daily practice or in planning (Anthea Coghlan).

I wanted to go on finding out how to change social work practice...so I used my improved curriculum vitae to get a job as a lecturer in a university...One thing led to another and I began to explore how to develop and to assess anti-racist and anti- discriminatory social work practice...So I started asking questions about the implementation of equal opportunity policies ...They didn't mind if I asked awkward questions about social work practice so long as I didn't ask the same questions about university practice (Nikki Cornwall).

It may have been the case that other contributors would have also experienced organisational resistance, and I am confident that this would have applied to both men and women, black and white. On the other hand it is probably no coincidence that organisational resistance was most strong and most felt by those promoting cooperative, egalitarian, feminist and anti-discriminatory ideas, faced with male dominated hierarchical and depressive institutions. In such circumstances, unless major changes take place, it is inevitable that many creative people, especially women and black people, will take their strengths and skills elsewhere.

There has then been a variety of ways in which undertaking practitioner research has been significant, in personal, conceptual and professional ways, at times meeting with organisational resistance, at other times meeting with organisational approval, at yet other times capturing the mood of a time with the selection of a particular topic. At another level these selections of observations by practitioner-researchers themselves reveal a changing research agenda and it is to that agenda finally to which I now turn.

The Changing Practitioner Research Agenda: From Professional Determination to Service Management

What is clear is that practitioner research was significant to those who completed it and that the research findings had significance always for the individual, always for their way of working, sometimes for the department and occasionally for the organisation and beyond. However the limits of influence, largely at the institutional level, probably both caught the mood of the period as well as stemmed from the changing nature of the learning contract.

In most cases these practitioner-researchers applied to undertake post-graduate research, *first* as committed individuals with a professional commitment to improving service (i.e. change) and *second* as an agency representative. The majority of topics chosen, including mine, were at the cutting edge of change about ways of delivering services to people who during the 1980s were universally described as clients. Each of these practitioner-researchers sought, and in some cases achieved, a measure of change to their professional practice and, when they returned to their workplace, to that of others. If one can generalise about social work research and the 1980s then it would be around the area of trying to improve professional practice and policies which aimed to improve outcomes, whilst also recognising the vital role that process contributes. If I am right, if only partially, then this key notion was also accompanied by a view that the policies and services could be improved *without* changing the nature of the institutions in which those policies were located. Of course with 'care in the community' legislation and other more recent legislation this has changed but my point about bureaucracies maintaining stability at a cost to innovation remains. It is hardly surprising then that those institutions were least likely during that period to take on major changes voluntarily. On the other hand it must be acknowledged that social policy development and implementation is an extraordinarily complex area and expecting any major change to institutions as a result of a single piece of practitioner research is quite frankly living in cloud cuckoo land. On the other hand the subsequent spread of influence arising from Bamford's research at departmental, institutional and national level suggests that in some circumstances such changes are possible. But why in that case and not others? Obviously one tempting answer is that the more academic the medium, the greater the circulation and acceptance of research findings. Yet Cornwall's academic experiences suggest that the nature of the research message being transmitted is at least as significant as the receiving equipment.

There are, of course, a range of factors determining whether/ how research findings are circulated and implemented. The list is potentially a long one. It includes the age, ethnic origin, gender, class dimensions of the researcher, but also their contacts, their grade in the organisation, the choice of research topic, the involvement by the researcher's employing authority (if there was one) in the choice of topic, the nature of the research, the institution involved and, not least of all, the national legislative/ social policy framework in which all activities are located. Of course, in a hierarchical organisation perhaps the least experienced staff member becoming a practitioner-researcher is ill-placed to influence policy decisions, although this will vary. Yet it must be remembered that for all the practitioner-researchers making their contribution, the personal significance of completing their research was considerable and it is inevitable that that valued experience subsequently influences theirs and others practices wherever they go, even if this is not directly related to the organisation to which they immediately returned.

The Changing Learning Contract

The learning contract for much of the practitioner research contained in this book was a two-way one (or in Maggie Riley's and Julia Phillipson's case a three-way one) between practitioner-researcher and the research institution's supervisor. In addition the research tended to focus on innovatory ideas and practices. The research itself seemed driven by a professional determination to 'go back', 'be better people' and 'to do more'. In the 1980s the research reinforced the personal and professional levels of significance. It was, as we have seen, at the institutional level at least in some cases where there were problems.

It is much more likely that future learning contracts will develop from business oriented managers and chief officers seeking more 'scientific' precision, financial efficiencies and outcome evaluation to meet the new demands of providing social care at a low cost in the United Kingdom. Specifically this will relate to the separation of the purchaser and the provider in community care, a point that Mike Carpenter made reference to earlier. In turn this will have a different, I fear detrimental, personal effect on those involved if I am right in assuming that monetary values (by which I mean finding ways of cutting costs and cutting services) will outweigh the human values of valuing individuals and their self-worth, whether service users or staff. Yet in the developing world of social work business, one in which I have myself been working for several years, the world of service managers, performance indicators and quality assurance, it is understandable and desirable that research becomes more a business oriented practice. One can only hope that this will also have some positive effect on those who use Social Services and the service users' movement, if I can call it that. Moves towards quality assurance and quality services must be welcome developments if proper resources can be made available. In practitioner research terms this new agenda for research will derive from a new learning contract which will be a three-way learning contract for practitioner-researchers. Indeed this is probably already the case. This will involve first the practitioner-researcher (probably evaluating an existing initiative), acting on behalf of the second party the employing agency, with the third party being the research supervisor. Indeed it may well be that for reasons of economy, albeit false ones in professional and academic terms, the research supervisor in future may not even by attached to an academic institution, but rather a freelancer. Thus there is the risk that the students' research topics and outcomes may be compromised by the fee being paid directly from the employer to the supervisor, or consultant. This type of three-way learning contract is a business/entrepreneurial contract. Another three-way learning contract it is hoped will be retained is a partnership/adult learning approach to research. This would reflect wider policy developments of agencies working closer together in part because professional and academic agencies are increasingly becoming financially interdependent. Another future practitioner research development is likely to be around the twin areas of anti-discriminatory and participatory social work research (involving service users as one of several parties) about which I have written elsewhere (Broad, 1993).[3] However this three-way learning contract, whether partnership/adult learning or business/entrepreneurial is likely to mean that certain sorts of research are less likely to be done in the future and that much innovative research is likely to become private property.

It is not that research itself must be innovatory or that it should research *only* innovatory practice. Rather the case is that research should and must always be a risky phenomenon in the sense that it critically questions what is and why is this so and suggests what could be in a rigorous way, free of censorship and to a high academic standard. Long may this be the case.

Footnotes
1. For further information on the (now closed) employment initiative for offenders in Inner London, see Pointing, J. (ed.) (1986) *Alternatives to Custody*. Oxford: Basil Blackwell.
2. My book *Punishment Under Pressure* (1991) provides an analysis of an organisation awkwardly positioned within a criminal justice system whose operation has consistently been found to be racist as well as sexist.
3. This article can be found in a separate volume with the revealing title *Rethinking Social Research* (Humphries, B. and Truman, C. (eds.) Aldershot: Avebury).

Appendix
Cranfield's Project Titles from 1978-1991

1978

The Effects of Professional Training in Social Work.

1980

Sex Roles and Social Work.

Mentally Handicapped Teenagers in Transition.

1981

Social Enquiry Reports.

1982

The Identification of Training Needs for Probation Officers.

Battered Women: An Appraisal of Social Policy.

Pastoral Support for Staff in Residential Schools.

1983

* *Adoption of Mentally Handicapped Children.*

Community Care for Late Adolescents: A Case Study.

* *Activity Groups in the Probation Service.*

The Observation and Assessment Process and the Information It Generates.

The Attitudes of Social Work Practitioners Towards Work with the Elderly.

Strategic Therapy.

* *The Probation Service and the Problem Drinker.*

* *Collective Working in the Personal Social Services.*

Independent Social Work in Child Care: A Study of a Controversial New Role.

Borough Associations for Disabled People.

1984

Care and Cooperation: A Study of Working Relationships Between Social Welfare Professionals.

* *Adult Training Centres and Open Employment.*

Community Care Services and Their Relevance to the Elderly.

Companion Animals in Foster Families.

Volunteers and the Elderly and Mentally Infirm.

An Evaluation of Induction Training for Senior Probation Officers.

Working with Parents and the Community: A Study of Two Family Centres.

* *Emergency Out-of-Hours Social Services.*

Specialist Team Work in a Social Services Department.

The Impact of the Troubles on the Workload of the Personal Social Services Department in Londonderry during 1978.

Implementing Change in Community Based Residential Child Care.

1985

* *The Personal Tutor in Social Work Education: A Qualitative Analysis.*

Social Work in Residential Practice.

The Training Needs of Care Assistants in Old People's Homes.
The Diffusion of Therapeutic Innovation in Social Work.
The Administrative Methods of Supervision within a Local Authority Social Services Department.

1986

* *Education: Whose Care?*
Do We Send Them Back to Homelessness?: The Probation Service Role with the No Fixed Abode Offender in a Large City.
Alternatives to Custody Under DHSS LAC (83)3 Initiatives.
Successful Community Tenure for Ex-Psychiatric Patients.

1987

Collaboration Between Health and Social Services.
* *Statementing: Assessment Decisions About Children.*
The Culture Shapes: A Study of Effective and Ineffective Leadership Behaviour in a Social Services Department.
Factors Influencing Decision-Making in Social Work.
Leadership and Management in Local Authority Residential Establishments for Children.
Residential Social Work: Fact or Fallacy.

1988

Disentangling the Voluntary Sector: A Study of Relationships Between Statutory and Voluntary Organisations in Leicester.
Assessment of Prospective Foster Parents: A Study of Intuitive Practice.
* *A Comparative Study of the Use of Day Centres by the Afro-Caribbeans of Oxford.*

1989

Family Placement and Access: Achieving Permanency for Children in Contact with Birth Parents.

1990

Decision-Making in the Assessment of Risk in Child Abuse Cases.
Effective Court Practice by the Probation Service.
Social Work Resources for Elderly People.
Respite Care for the Elderly.
Management Information in a Social Services Department.

1991

* *Parenting Children with Physical Impairments: The Parents' Perspective.*
Old Age - Threat or Promise: The Situations of People aged 75 and Over in Two Parts of East Herts.
Accomplishment in Adversity: A Study of Practitioner Learning in Social Work.
* *Old Age Abuse.*
* *Mental Health Social Work.*
Addiction Services and Politics.
Out of Sight Out of Mind; Kids on the Merry Go Round - Workers in the Dark. A Study of Children in Care Placed Outside of a Local Authority.

* indicates article in this book.

Contributors

David Bamford is Head of Department of Applied Social Studies, University of Ulster. He has been involved in social work education for over 20 years. He trained as a psychiatric social worker at the University of Leeds, qualifying in 1970, and since then has been based in Northern Ireland while having involvement in all parts of the British Isles in social work education through external examining, conferences, publications, etc. His thesis on *The Personal Tutor in Social Work Education* was published as a book (Cranfield Press, 1987). David is married with two children and lives adjacent to the Jordanstown campus of the University of Ulster.

David Bowen's future as a teacher was very early on diverted into social work, mostly with children and their families. He now combines the two interests as Principal Education Welfare Officer for Dorset.

Bob Broad is Development Manager (Training, Research and Policy), Royal Philanthropic Society, a voluntary organisation based in Brasted, Kent helping young people at risk in London and the South East. Prior to that he was a Probation Officer in London, interspersed with periods in social work lecturing at the London School of Economics and the University of Central London. Since completing his MSc at Cranfield, he gained his doctorate from Middlesex University in 1988, based on an investigative study into inner city probation work. He has also written several articles, done consultancy work and directed in-service training courses at Cranfield for Probation Officers. He edited *Enquiries into Community Probation Work* (DSP Publications, Cranfield,1988) and has published *Punishment Under Pressure: The Probation Service in the Inner City* (Jessica Kingsley, 1991). He is especially interested in clients' rights, quality and equality of service delivery, and worker rights and accountability.

Mike Carpenter, a career social worker, entered Social Service management in 1969 and during the ensuing years had an involvement with all aspects of Social Services ranging from the management of social work through to day and residential care. Following a year out to study for the MSc at Cranfield, Mike became Director of Social Services in the early 80s and in the last three years has added to that the strategic responsibility for managing Housing Services within his authority.

Anthea Coghlan has practiced as a social worker since 1987, both as a fieldworker and in senior roles, in a great variety of settings. She is especially interested in the broader common issues in the provision of Social Services. For the last ten years she has been fortunate in having the opportunity to work in a multidisciplinary team providing a service to children who have developmental problems and to their families. In 1991, she completed her study, *Parenting Children with Physical Impairments: The Parents' Perspective* for which she was awarded the MPhil at Cranfield. In co-operation with parents of children who have disabilities, she has continued to disseminate her learning through teaching and practice and she is working on the development of a model of multidisciplinary practice. She is Care Manager of children with disabilities in Northamptonshire.

Nicki Cornwell moved via research from extensive practice experience to be a Lecturer in Social Work at the University of Bath. She is concerned by the discrepancy between theory and practice. She has published research on 'statementing' and several articles on social work. She is now Centre Manager of KIDS, Camden, London.

Colin Fletcher graduated in Social Sciences, qualified in Industrial Administration and his doctorate is about Managerial Stress. He has held research contracts with the DHSS, British Steel Corporation and DES. In 1981 he joined Cranfield to develop practitioner research in the public and voluntary sectors. He initiated a Practitioner Research PhD programme in 1984. He has published books and articles on education and research and edited a book series on 'Innovations in Education'. His interests are in applied research methods, core skills in research training; leadership, policy and practice in the non-profit sectors particularly in education and voluntary organisations. He is Professor of Educational Research, University of Wolverhampton.

Eric Knapman has been an Assistant Chief Probation Officer since 1972. Between 1984-1991 he was Chair of the Northamptonshire Council on Addiction and has had a strong interest in addictions since working as a liaison officer to a drug clinic in London between 1969-1972. An avid learner, he studied with the Open University prior to attending Cranfield in 1980-82 and, more recently, completed an MBA at Leicester Polytechnic.

Catherine Macaskill is a Lecturer in Post Qualifying Studies, Department of Health and Social Work, Aberdeen University. Initially trained as a teacher and then as a social worker, she has extensive experience in the specialist areas of adoption, fostering and community care for children with disabilities. Her Cranfield thesis *Against the Odds: Adopting Mentally Handicapped Children* has been published (British Agencies for Adoption and Fostering, 1988). Three years later, she published a further study entitled *Adopting or Fostering a Sexually Abused Child* (Batsford, 1991). She has used this study as the basis for providing in-service training in child sexual abuse for foster carers, adopters and social workers.

Barbara Mallon is a senior social worker with extensive experience in working with a combination of different client groups. For the last six years she has specialised in working with adults (elderly and physically disabled people). Her concern for elderly people and their carers led to her carrying out research into abuse of elderly people for which she has been awarded an MPhil at Cranfield. Her other interests include: the supervision of students, the use of theory in social work practice and the role of carers caring for dependent adults,

Richard Mitchell qualified as social worker in 1970. Later he trained at the Tavistock as a consultant to working groups and he is a practicing psychotherapist. He has worked in a variety of social work settings but his main interest lies in working with the mentally distressed. For the last 15 years he has been employed by the London Borough of Barnet and is currently a senior management officer. He has helped establish and develop Barnet's well known multidisciplinary crisis intervention and community mental health service. The practice of the mental health social work team within that service formed the basis of his MPhil thesis.

Julia Phillipson and Maggie Riley used to work for the National Institute for Social Work and in community development in Milton Keynes respectively. Both now work as independent consultants in the public and voluntary sectors. They enjoy collaborative working, working with women - especially each other; postcards, flowers, poetry and colour. We also believe in working in ways that 'shift' traditional practice as our undertaking of our joint MPhil shows.

Alan Stanton practised as a solicitor, before switching to social work, and then into research. His thesis on collective teamwork was published as *Invitation to Self Management* (Dabhand Press, 1989). He has since edited an Oxfam book on research methods for development workers, and is currently involved in restructuring local government from the bottom up.

Tony Stocks' education, like Oscar Wilde's, was interrupted by a period at school, having left at 15 with no formal qualifications and no job. In 1981-82 Tony was appointed as research assistant to John Paley, Cranfield Institute, the research being funded by the DHSS. Less than one year after the DHSS received their report (*Adult Training Centres and Open Employment*) Central Government announced that they were not to build any more Adult Training Centres in England and Wales. After Tony completed his Masters Degree he went on to study for his PhD at the Institute of Social and Applied Psychology, University of Kent at Canterbury. Upon his return from University he worked with the ever increasing population of homeless people in Cambridge, where he completed his 'education'. Tony now works as a manager of a private day unit with people who have profound learning difficulties.

Grace Thomas was a professional teacher who had a mid-career change into social work and is a Sociology graduate of Lancaster University 1976-79. She read the MPhil in Social Policy at Cranfield Institute of Technology 1987-88. Grace's MA/CQSW thesis *Coping with Ageing: Afro-Caribbean Elderly Women* has since been published (Warwick University, 1990).

Simon Villette is Assistant Education Officer with Northamptonshire LEA. He is closely involved in the implementation of special education policies and the Children Act, having taught in both education and Social Services settings. He has particular experience in training people for managing change.

Bernard Webb is beginning his 11th year as Assistant Co-ordinator in the Emergency Duty Team, Lothian Region Social Work Department. To overcome the stresses of Local Authority social work, he has for some years operated an antiquarian and out-of-print bookselling business, with his wife.

References

Bales, R.F. (1967) 'A Set of Categories For The Analysis of Small Group Interaction' in Mills, T.M. *The Sociology of Small Groups*. Prentice Hall.

Bennett, P. and Lupton, S. (1982) *Social Work and Alcohol Dependence*. University of East Anglia in Association with *Social Work Today*.

Berger, P.L. and Luckmann, T. (1966) *The Social Construction of Reality*. Doubleday.

Berman-Rossi, T. (1988), 'Theoretical Orientations of Social Work Practice Teachers: An Analysis, *Journal of Social Work in Education*, 24(1), pp.50-59.

Bramley, W. (1977 *Personal Tutoring in Higher Education*. Guildford: University of Surrey.

Breckman and Adelman (1988) *Strategies for Helping Victims of Elder Mistreatment*. California; Sage.

Broad, B. (1982) *Activity Groups in the Probation Service*. Unpublished MSc Thesis, Cranfield Institute of Technology.

Broad, B. (1991) *Punishment Under Pressure: The Probation Service in the Inner City*. London: Jessica Kingsley.

Broad, B. (1991a) 'The Use and Abuses of Professional Power in Social Work Groups', Paper for the 1st European Groupwork Symposium, Imperial College, London University, 18-19 July 1991, *Symposium Report*. London: Whiting and Birch Ltd.

Broad, B. (1993), 'Anti Discriminatory Research: Some Perennial Problems and Possible Solutions' in Humphreys B. and Truman C. *Rethinking Social Research*. Aldershot: Avebury.

Brown, G.W. and Birley, J.L.T. (1968) 'Crisis and Life Changes and the Onset of Schizophrenia', *Journal of Health and Social Behaviour*, 9, pp.203-214.

Busfield, J. (1986) *Managing Madness*. London: Hutchinson.

Campbell, D.T. (1974) 'Evolutionary Epistemology' in Schilpp, P.A. (ed.) *The Philosophy of Karl Popper*. Open Court.

CCETSW (1990) *The Requirements for Post Qualifying Education and Training in the Personal Social Services: A Framework for Continuing Professional Development*. Paper 31. London: CCETSW.

Charkin, N.F. (1986) 'The Practice-Research Relationship: An Organisational Link', *Social Service Review*, 60(2), pp.241-250.

Clarke, A.D.B. and Hermelin, B.F. (1966) 'Adult Imbeciles and their Abilities and Trainability', *The Lancet*, 2, pp.337-339.

Crolley, T. (1982) *The Identification of Training Needs for Probation Officers*. MSc Thesis, Cranfield Institute of Technology, Social Policy Group.

Cunningham, C. and Davis, H. (1985) *Working with Parents: Frameworks for Collaboration*. Milton Keynes: Open University Press.

DHSS (1971) *Better Services for the Mentally Handicapped*. H.M.S.O., London.

DHSS (1971) *Community Homes Design Guide, Advisory Council on Child Care*. London: HMSO.

DHSS (1980) *Homelessness and Strategy for Research on Alcoholism*. Addictions Liaison Group. London: DHSS.

Davies, I.P. and Reid, W.J. (1988) 'Event Analysis in Clinical Practice and Process Research', *Social Casework*, 69(5), pp.298-306.

Davies, M. (1974) *Social Work in the Environment*. Home Office Research Unit Report, HMSO.

De Roos, Y.S. (1990) 'The Development of Practice Wisdom through Human Problem-Solving Processes', *Social Service Review*, 64(2), pp.276-287.

Douglas, J.W.B. and Ross, J.M. (1965) 'The Effects of Absence on Primary School Performance', *British Journal of Educational Psychology*, 35, pp.28-39.

Eaton, M.J. (1979) 'A Study of Some Factors Associated with the Early Identification of Persistent Absenteeism', *Educational Review*, 31(3), pp.233-242.

Farewell, T. (1976) 'Crisis Intervention', *Nursing Mirror*, September, pp.60-61.

Ferguson and Beck (1983) 'HALF - A Tool to Assess Elder Abuse Within the Family', *Geriatric Nursing*, Sept-Oct, pp.301-304).

Fleming, I. (1978) 'Mentally Handicapped School-Leavers: Their Assessment and Placement', *APEX*, 6(1), pp.23-26.

Fletcher, C. (1972) *Beneath the Surface: An Account of Three Styles of Social Research*. Routledge and Kegan Paul.

Fletcher, C. (1980) 'The Sutton Centre Profile' in Burgess, T. and Adams, E. (eds.) *Outcomes of Education*. Macmillan Education.

Galloway, D. (1976) 'Persistent Unjustified Absence from School', *Trends*, 4, pp.22-27.

Gelman, S.R. and Wardell, P.J. (1988) 'Who's Responsible?: The Field Liability Dilemma', *Journal of Social Work Education*, 24(1), pp.70-78.

Gitterman, A. 'Teaching Students to Connect Theory and Practice', *Social Work with Groups*, 1(1-2), pp.33-41.

Glaser, B.G. and Strauss, A.L. (1967) *The Discovery of Grounded Theory*. New York: Aldine Press.

Goldstein, H. (1990) 'The Knowledge Base of Social Work Practice: Theory, Wisdom, Analogue or Art?', *Families in Society*, 71(1), pp.32-43.

Gordon, S., O'Connor, N. and Tizard J. (1954) 'Some Effects of Incentives on the Performance of Imbeciles on a repetitive Task', *American Journal of Mental Deficiency*, 60, pp.371-377.

Gould, N. (1989), 'Reflective Learning for Social Work Practice', *Social Work Education*, 8(2), pp.9-19.

Grant, G.W., Moore, B. and Whelan, E. (1973), 'Assessing the Work Needs and Work Performance of Mentally Handicapped Adults', *British Journal of Mental Subnormality*, 19, pp.71-79.

Grimmett, P.P. and Erickson, G.L. (1988) *Reflection in Teacher Education*. Teachers College Press.

Grunsell, R. (1978) *Born to be Invisible: The Story of a School for Truants*. London: Macmillan Educational.

HMSO (1970) *A Guide to Adoption Practice*. HMSO: London.

HMSO (1971) *Better Services for the Mentally Handicapped*. HMSO: London.

HMSO (1979) *Report of the Committee of Enquiry into Mental Handicap Nursing and Care*. The Jay Report. Volumes 1 and 2. HMSO: London.

References

HMSO (1979) *A Better Life: Report on Services for the Mentally Handicapped in Scotland*. Scottish Home and Health Department and Scottish Education Department.

Harper, J. (1984) 'Out There in the Field', *Community Care*, 5 January.

Hartmann, A. (1990) 'Education for Direct Practice', *Families in Society*, 71(1), pp.44-50.

Heraud, B. (1981) *Training for Uncertainty*. RKP.

Ho, M.K. (1975), 'Implications of Teacher-Student Relationships in Social Work Education', *Journal of Social Work*, 11(1).

Hobes, M. (1984), 'Crisis Intervention in theory and Practice: A Selective Review', *British Journal of Medical Psychology*, 57, pp.23-34.

Hotaling, Finkelhor, Kirkpatrick and Straus (1988) *Family Abuse and Its Consequences*. Sage.

Hourd (1972) *Relationship in Learning*. London: Heinemann Educational Books.

Howe, E.G. (1965) *Cure or Heal? A Study of Therapeutic Experience*. Allen and Unwin.

Jones, M. (1990) 'Understanding Social Work: A Matter of Interpretation', *British Journal of Social Work*, 20(3), pp.181-196.

Jones, M.J. (1988) 'Instruments and Expressive Behaviours in Time, Cultural Differences in Temporal Perspectives' in McGrath, J. (ed.) *The Social Psychology of Time*. Beverley Hills: Sage.

Kaplin, H.I. and Sadock, J. (1988) *Synopsis of Psychiatry*. Baltimore: Williams and Wilkins.

Kelly, G. (1955) *The Psychology of Personal Constructs*. Volumes 1 and 2. W.W. Norton.

Kessell, N. and Walton, H. (1979) *Alcoholism*. London: Penguin.

Levy, C.S. (1976) *Social Work Ethics*. New York: Human Sciences Press.

Litz, T. (1987) 'The Effective Treatment of Schizophrenic Patients', *Journal of Nervous and Mental Diseases*, 157(8), pp.447-449.

Mildenberger and Wessman (1986) 'Abuse and Neglect of Elderly Persons by Family Members (A Special Communication)', *Physical Therapy*, 66(4), pp.537-539.

Moreno, J.L. (1960) *The Sociometry Reader*. Illinois, USA: Free Press of Glenco.

O'Hagan, K. (1986) *Crisis Intervention in Social Services*. Basingstoke and London: Macmillan.

Pillemer and Finkelhor (1988) 'The Prevalence of Elder Abuse: A Random Sample Survey', *The Gerontologist*, 28(1).

Preston, M.S. (1989) 'A Contractual Approach to Practice Teaching', *Social Work Education*, 8(3), pp.3-15.

Radin, N. (1989) 'School of Social Work Practice: Past, Present and Future Trends', *Social Work in Education*, 11(4), pp.213-225.

Richan, W.C. and Mendelsohn, A.R. (1973) 'Social Work - The Unloved Profession', *New Viewpoints*. New York.

Roskies, E. (1972) *Abnormality and Normality: The Mothering of Thalidomide Children*. Cornell University Press.

Royal College of Psychiatrists (1979) *Alcohol and Alcoholism*. Report of a Special Committee. London: Tavistock Publications.

Rumgay, J. (1988) 'Teaching Social Work Practice: A Partnership Between College and Field', *Practice*, 2(4), pp.334-345.

Rushton, J.H. (1976) *A Study of the Individual Tutorial in Social Work Education*. Unpublished MSc Thesis, University of Leeds.

Rutter, M., Maughan, B., Mortimort, P., Ouston, J. with Smith A. (1979) *Fifteen Thousand Hours*. London: Optu Books.

Schon, D. (1987) *Educating the Reflective Practitioner*. Jossey-Bass.

Schon, D.A. (1983) *The Reflective Practitioner: How Professionals Think in Action*. Basic Books.

Sengstocki and Hwalek (1987), 'A Review and Analysis of Measures for the Identification of Elder Abuse', *Journal of Gerontological Social Work*, 10 (3-4).

Shani, A.B. and Bushe, G.R. (1987) 'Visionary Action Research: A Consultation Process Perspective', *Consultation*, 6(1), pp.3-19.

Sowers, H.Q. and Thyer, B.A. (1985) 'Teaching Social Work Practice: A Review and Analysis of Empirical Research, *Journal of Social Work Education*, 21(3), pp.5-15.

Stacey, M. (1991) *Parents and Teachers Together*. Open University Press.

Starr, J.M. (1981) 'Adolescents and Resistance to Schooling', *Youth and Society*, 13(2), pp.198-227.

Staub, B.S. (1988) 'Theoreticians and Practitioners of Social Work', *Schweizerische Zeitschrift für Soziologie*, 14(3), pp.445-468.

Strauss, A. (1987) *Qualitative Analysis for Social Scientists*. Cambridge: Cambridge University Press.

Syson, L. (1981) *Learning to Practice*. London: CCETSW.

Teigiser, K.S. and Chambon, A. (1989) 'From Concepts to Practice', *Journal of Teaching in Social Work*, 3(1), pp.117-130.

Tizard, J. and Loos, F.M. (1954) 'The Learning of Spathal Relations Test by Adult Imbeciles', *American Journal of Mental Deficiency*, 59, pp.85-90.

Tropp, E. (1970) 'Authenticity in Teacher-Student Communication' in *Teaching and Learning in Social Work Education*. New York: Council on Social Work Education, p.25.

Warnock Report (1978) *Special Educational needs: Report of the Committee of Enquiry into the Education of Handicapped Children and Young People*. Cmd, 7212.

Weinbach, R.W. and Rubin, A. (eds.) *Teaching Social Work Research*. New York: Council on Social Work Education.

Whelan, E. and Speake, B. (1977) *A Set of Habilitation Packages For The Use With Mentally Handicapped and Developmentally Delayed Adults and Adolescents*. Habilitation Technology Project, Hester Adrian Research Centre, University of Manchester.

Whelan, E. and Speake, B. (1977) *Adult Training Centres in England and Wales*. Manchester: National Association of Teachers of the Mentally Handicapped.

Whitaker, D.S. and Archer, J.L. (1989) *Research by Social Workers: Capitalising on Experience*. Study 9. London: CCETSW.

Wood, K.M. (1980) *Experiences in Teaching The Practitioner-Researcher Model*.